YAMPA VALLEY'S
LOST
EGERIA PARK

RITA HEROLD

THE
History
PRESS

Published by The History Press
Charleston, SC
www.historypress.com

First published 2020

Manufactured in the United States

ISBN 9781467143998

Library of Congress Control Number: 2019951842

CONTENTS

INTRODUCTION

When I was young, my great-uncles Tom and Ben Laughlin and my grandfather Herb Moore told me about their experiences and their lives in early Egeria Park.

The Laughlin family came into the valley in the mid-1880s; Tom was four years old, and Ben was ten. When they were older, both of those fellows enjoyed being around children, and they were articulate tellers of tales. Herb Moore first came into the Yampa area in 1887, and he also loved to share his knowledge and tell the stories.

Because of that background, I started collecting those accounts and the history of the area. I have also been very fortunate that my father, Francis Moore (son of Herb Moore and Bertha Laughlin), grew up in South Routt County and had marvelous memories of the past. When this writing was started, Francis was still alive and was still able to tell of many of the past events of the valley. Between 1999 and 2009, Francis wrote down some of his memories. I have included various narratives of his in this book.

There is not a formal history of Egeria Park, but several different people have written manuscripts of their lives or the life of a family member, and they shared some of that information. Some of those descriptions and incidents are also included here.

The old photographs have come from different sources. Some are from my own family. Some have been shared. When I was teaching classes on South Routt History for the Colorado Northwest Community College, many of the students had deep roots and interests in Routt County; they willingly shared their views and memorabilia.

I wish to thank all who have been so helpful in adding to the knowledge of the area and given me encouragement in compiling this information, especially my family.

1
EARLY EGERIA PARK

E geria Park—just where was Egeria Park? What was Egeria Park?
According to David S. Gray, the boundaries of the park in the
1880s included the entire upper Yampa River valley.[1] He included
the area from Gore Pass to the Flattops, then north to south from the
area that now contains Stagecoach Reservoir to Red Dirt Pass south of
Toponas. Old-timers such as Tom Laughlin and H.E. Moore defined
Egeria Park as the area surrounding Toponas and on down the valley,
including present-day Phippsburg. They did not include the Stagecoach
Reservoir area. So even in the early days, Egeria Park had no exact
boundaries. Egeria Park was divided loosely into two parts, with Upper
Egeria taking in the land surrounding Toponas down the valley to an
east–west line near Finger Rock. Lower Egeria encompassed the valley
from Finger Rock north to include Phippsburg. Lower Egeria also
included the South Hunt Creek drainage.

The streams in the Upper Egeria basin, Egeria Creek, King Creek,
Toponas Creek and so on all flow southward to reach the Colorado River in
Eagle County. The streams in Lower Egeria all enter the Yampa River. The
Yampa River joins with the Green River near the Utah line west of Craig;
hence, the water from Lower Egeria finally intersects the Colorado River
near Moab, Utah. This high mountain park drops in elevation from 8,284
feet in Toponas, 7,881 feet in Yampa, to 7438 feet in Phippsburg.[2] The drop
in elevation occurs within a distance of about 20 miles.

The name *Egeria* comes from Roman mythology. Egeria was the goddess of wells and springs, and she was reputed to be both beautiful and wise.[3] However, which person first called this lush mountain valley "Egeria" is disputed.

Lulita Crawford Pritchett found an article written by James Crawford in an *Inter-Mountain* newspaper dated 1889. The article asserted, "Captain E.L. Berthoud named it in 1861 when he made his exploration of the range and regions west for the U.S. Government."

On September 14, 1941, the *Steamboat Pilot* included a letter to the editor written by Billy Whipple. Whipple wrote the following story about the naming of Egeria Park:

> *Egeria Park was named by Sir George Gore, Irish explorer and hunter, whose name is perpetuated in the names, Gore Pass and Gore Canyon. He was camped at the entrance of Egeria Park, near Toponas, in 1879 and he said at that time, he had named Egeria park several years before that, on one of his previous trips. He only remained in the camp a short time owing to the Indian outbreak at Meeker.*

Dave Gray gave this version about the naming of the valley: James Scott of the Iron Spring Ranch, a friend of Governor Routt, claimed that Governor Routt explained, "I visited that unnamed country one time crossing over the Gore range. I reached the top of Spruce Hill, when the sun was low in the west. I thought it the most beautiful picture I had ever seen and I said, 'I name this park Egeria', meaning beautiful."[4]

Jan Leslie's research showed Louis Berthoud and Jim Bridger went through the mountain passes to establish the place for a wagon road to run from Denver to Salt Lake City.[5] At the time (1861), Berthoud was also writing for the *Rocky Mountain News*, and he claimed that "the name [Egeria] was suggested by Governor Gilpin."

The first inhabitants of this area left no written records. Folsom points found in both the Flattop area and on Rabbit Ears indicate that prehistoric peoples used the Yampa Valley long before recorded history. There have been at least two different archaeological findings of prehistoric tribes in the Yampa area that predate the Ute, Shoshone, Sioux and others.

One finding was of a preserved mummy-type grave. These remains were found around 1925 by two teachers from the Yampa School.[6] This site was about half a mile west of the smaller of the two Laughlin Buttes. M.E. Bouton was the principal of the school, and Mr. O.E. Baird was the sixth

Evening in Egeria Park. *Author's collection.*

and seventh grade teacher. Francis Moore was not sure which one actually found the remains, but the educators worked together to remove them and send them into the Museum of Colorado History in Denver.

It is unknown if the mummy was ever on display, but it became a part of the museum's "basement collection" and may have been included in the sweeping return of artifacts to different tribes in the 1980s and '90s.

The second site of archaeological significance was at the base of the rock at the larger of the two Laughlin Buttes. In the mid-1960s, John Miles and Rick Moore were playing in a small depression by the rock when they found a few bones and several small "seed" beads. The beads were hand-drilled turquoise. Those artifacts were sent to Denver. They were supposedly dated as premodern Native American, and the bones were evidently of two different people.

Americans of today tend to think of the United States as starting in 1776. We did object to England's rule at that time, but it was not until thirteen years later in 1789 that George Washington started his first term in office as president. It was not until twenty-five years later, in 1801, that Thomas Jefferson, the second president, started to include more area into our young country.

The people of that time had a better knowledge of the interior of the United States than one might think. The Louisiana Purchase occurred in 1803. The Lewis and Clark Expedition was the official exploration at that time, but there were also individual explorers and trappers that entered the mountains of Colorado.

Moreover, gold was discovered at South Park in Colorado. That information apparently became "lost" in the government papers. Was it just not important enough to look for gold at that time? Did they think there was not enough gold to bother with? Was it too far into the wilderness to be important? Or, perhaps, the United States did not want the Spanish to think that there was treasure to be found north of Santa Fe. Whatever the reason, the finding of gold was not publicized at the time. In 1805, Baptise LaLande and James Purcell explored, hunted and traded in the mountainous region of Colorado and were possibly the first Americans to see what would become the thirty-eighth state.[7] Actually, Purcell related finding gold in South Park to Zebulon Pike in 1807. In 1806, Zebulon Pike started exploring some of the Colorado region, but then he became a political prisoner in Santa Fe during the winter of 1807. During his incarceration, he recorded a variety of information about Colorado.

Purcell was also documented as James Pursley. James Pursley traveled to New Mexico from Saint Louis hunting along the way. His travels included trips into the Arkansas and Colorado River Basins. In New Mexico in 1807, Pike met fellow American Pursley/Purcell, and the former recalled that he traded with South Platte Indians as early as 1805. He also went with them into South Park and found gold flakes. Most of the older sources, such as *The Story of Colorado*, seem to favor the "Pursley" spelling.[8]

The Spanish were possessive of the land they claimed—it is quite possible that other hunters and traders were reluctant to admit that they had traveled into the Spanish territory that became Colorado.

When the early explorers and trappers came into the Yampa Valley, they found that many different tribes enjoyed this area. The Arapahoe, the Cheyenne, the Sioux, the Shoshone and especially the Ute Nations were all listed as living in the area during the 1800s. These tribes were not always friendly toward one another. There were various fights recorded between the different tribes. During the last half of the 1800s, the Utes were documented as being in the Egeria Park region more often than the other tribes. The treaty of 1848 included part of present-day Routt County in the lands bestowed on the Utes.

Most early trappers did not write about their excursions into the Rocky Mountains; that honor was left for others to tell their story.

In the 1830s and 1840s, after completing their schooling, many financially secure young men from the United States came west to have grand adventures before settling into business. (At the time, virtually all the land west of the Mississippi River was considered wilderness.) Some of these men kept journals or wrote books when they returned east.

One such writer was E. Willard Smith, who went to school in New York for engineering. When he graduated at twenty-three, his father gave him a blank journal before he went west in which Smith described his western trip. The following notes show insight into what was happening in the Yampa Valley at that time.

Smith left Independence on August 6, 1839 with "Messrs. Vasquez & Sublette."[9] On September 13, he arrived at the fort of Messrs. Sublette & Vasquez, situated on the South Fork of the river Platt. On September 16, Smith left with a Mr. Thompson and Mr. Craig and their families to go to "a trading Fort at Brown's Hole, a valley on the west side of the mountain."

They traveled up the Cache-la-Poudre River, across the Laramie Fork, then through the Buffalo Bull Pen (North Park). On September 25, they spent the evening encamped on a ridge called "the Divide." (This would have been either Buffalo Pass or possibly Ute Pass.)

In his journal, Smith related finding a campsite on the Snake River where a group of whites fought with the Sioux and where at least four horses had been killed. Two days later, Smith recorded the following: "29th. To-day we left Snake River and about noon came across Indian signs. We supposed there must have been about forty Indians, probably a war party of Sioux that had passed but two or three hours previous to our coming. If they had seen us, we might have had a fight."

The party went on to Brown's Hole, where Smith found that Kit Carson claimed the honor of fighting a battle against the Sioux on the Snake River. While Smith's party was encamped in Brown's Hole, "about twenty lodges of Snake Indians [Shoshone] joined them."

Smith continued his log with a description of a trip into Utah where he observed some Utes at a fort there. Smith's log was written for his own use, not necessarily for publication as were some of the concurrent logs written by other young men about their western escapades. (After Smith returned to New York he did publish the notes from his journal.)

The same year Smith was visiting the Yampa Valley, a group of five people, exploring on their way to Oregon, traveled through western Colorado.[10] One of them, Thomas Jefferson Farnham, wrote a journal and then a book about his "western adventures." Farnham was a lawyer from Vermont but was living in Peoria, Illinois.[11]

Farnham and his four companions continued up the Arkansas River into the mountains. A Kentuckian named Kelly, who had spent twelve years in the service of the American Fur Company, was employed as a guide. They turned northwest over the Park Range and trekked to the headwaters of the Yampa River. Here they came upon a log cabin built by their guide, Kelly, several years before. In it, he had defended a sick companion from an Indian attack. The travelers continued their journey down the Yampa River. On August 12, they found "the humble but hospitable" Fort Davy Crockett.

Fort Davy Crockett was in what is today called Brown's Park. That area, then called Brown's Hole, was one of the first places settled in western Colorado.

Most of the trappers who came into the Yampa Valley in the young days of the United States did not record their own adventures. Between 1820 and 1845, people such as William Ashley, Kit Carson, Jim Baker, Peg-Leg Smith, Jim Bridger and Thomas Fitzpatrick were all known to visit the Bear River area—what we know today as the Yampa Valley. One challenge in sorting out the information from that time is the fact that there were several streams and rivers called "Bear River" throughout the West. When someone said he camped on the Bear River, was it the Colorado Bear River or was it the one in Wyoming or perhaps Montana?

When starting his Rocky Mountain Fur Company, William Ashley encouraged and worked with the "free trappers." Evidently, many of these men spent a short time in one place before moving to another area for a while. Trapping seemed to be a way to make enough money for supplies. These men enjoyed seeing new country, though some preferred specific locales. Another favorite pastime seemed to be horse stealing. "Horse stealing excursions were a business which the trapper looked upon as perfectly legitimate when it was properly directed."[12]

The mountain men and their Indian allies made a business of going to California on horse thieving raids. In one raid, they picked up "five or six hundred" Spanish horses and returned on a northerly route to the Green River area. Bill Williams, Joe Meek and Peg-Leg Smith all felt that taking horses from the Californians was a great way to spend a few months. Their favorite escape route was to travel through Utah north of the Grand Canyon into the Green River area of Wyoming. They then went through different valleys of Colorado to Bent's Fort, where they found a market for the stolen horses.

Sir Saint George Gore, the Eighteenth Baronet of Manor Gore from the County Donegal, Ireland, traveled on a hunting trip into Colorado. However, detailed information about his time in Egeria Park is vague. A great deal of Lord Gore's time in Colorado seems to be legend rather than verifiable facts. Physically, he was described as "a fine built, stout, light-haired and resolute looking man."[13] In the summer and fall of 1854, Gore came from Wyoming through North Park and on into Middle Park.

Jim Bridger was Gore's chief scout and knew the area well. Bridger had been in the area many times, and his wife was Ute. He had friends and relatives among the Yampa Utes.

Leaving most of the wagons and men, Bridger led Gore west from Middle Park toward the Yampa Valley. When Bridger guided the Gore party into the valley, they found a band of Yampa Utes led by Chief White Eye. Located not too far from the present town of Yampa, this was a camp of more than a hundred lodges; it included a few lodges of Shoshones. With the large group of Gore's men and wagons going into North and Middle Parks, the Utes would have known about Gore's hunting trip and his decimation of the different game animals. "At the Yampa village in that fall of 1854, Chief

White Eye respectfully requested that Lord Gore and Jim Bridger venture no further down the valley on their hunting expedition."[14] The parting was friendly, and presents were exchanged. Gore and his party returned into Wyoming by the same route they had come.

Since Jim Bridger was well acquainted with the Utes in the area, it is plausible he had a rough idea of where this band camped. Also, Bridger could have guessed what the Utes' reaction to the Gore hunting party would be. It is possible Bridger did not like the wholesale slaughter of the animals or the invasion of the valley either.

In the Steamboat Springs area, the first settlers claimed their homesteads in 1875 before the Yampa Utes were removed from Routt County. There were several trappers in the southern part of the county before 1881. These fellows were not considered permanent residents, as they did not stay in the area year-round. These trappers included Jack Hill, Al Martin, Jim Bennett, Hank Veach and Tom Smith; undoubtedly, there were others.

There were other nonnative people in the Yampa Valley, but we cannot verify those who left no written records. We can only speculate about who they were. Were they trappers or mountain men not as well known as those listed earlier? Were they early Spanish residents trying to expand their holdings? Were they Latter-day Saint (Mormon) settlers? The following story refers to information recorded by James Crawford after he and his family had observed some ruins. The antiquity of the finds seems to indicate that people were in the area before the Mormons' exodus across the western United States. The following article appeared in the golden anniversary edition of the *Steamboat Pilot*:

> *The first settlers at Steamboat Springs probably will remain a mystery, for the only record they left of their occupancy was silent as to the owners. The first visitors to leave a record—found on the south side of the river, near a little clump of cottonwoods, 50 yards from the river bank and almost opposite Eighth Street—an adobe fort, some 20 feet square, showing great age. In 1875, the walls were still standing several feet high and portholes therein showed that the structure was built for defense Up until a few years ago, the old walls could be traced, but when the railroad track was graded, all of the evidences were destroyed. In the green timber near the sulfur cave the first settlers to leave a record found the remains of a decayed log cabin, possibly of the same age as the adobe fort and this showed evidence of great age, for timber does not decay rapidly in this dry atmosphere. Another evidence of the former occupancy and throwing some light on the past was*

Beaver Pond in Upper Egeria Park, circa 1910. *Courtesy of Yampa-Egeria Museum; photo by Clark LaFon.*

Drawing of a cottonwood tree with a broken ox bow. *Author's depiction.*

a giant cottonwood tree close to the riverbank and directly opposite Tenth Street. This tree had been a giant among its fellows and had died, partly decayed and been blown down. While it was still growing, somebody had bored a hole into its side and placed therein a broken ox bow, evidently for the purpose of hanging something thereon. The scar had healed; the broken ox bow had almost grown to be a part of the tree. The tree had completed its growth, was now prostrate and partially decayed, but contained evidence that showed indisputably the visit of early travelers, and that he had wagons and oxen here.[15]

Lulita Crawford Pritchett recorded a somewhat similar story in her book *Maggie by My Side.* Yarmonite, a Ute friend of the Crawford family, told them this story in his broken English:

When he was a little boy—so high—his father had been chief. The big Ute camp was on the south bank of Bear River, and three white men had goods to trade with the Indians. One day a war party of Arapahos sneaked over from North Park and attacked the Ute camp. Since the invaders were on a hill and could shoot down into the tepees, they had the advantage. The Utes fought back. The battle raged three days. Yarmonite's father was killed, and the Utes were getting the worst of it. Under cover of darkness on the third night they took the chief's body and moved down the river and the three white men moved with them.[16]

Yarmonite remembered this because every year he made a ceremonial journey back to the spot where his father was killed. Reasoning that Yarmonite was then sixty-five years of age and had been perhaps eight years old at the time of the battle, James Crawford figured the adobe fort could have been built around 1818.

One interesting part of this find was the equipment for oxen. Oxen were steady at hauling freight and pulling heavy loads; they did not panic in swamps or bogs, but they were not as fast as horses. The Indians, the early trappers and the explorers favored the faster horses. Were the people hoping to use the oxen to skid logs out for their homes or for a fort? Perhaps they hoped to use them to plow fields. The evidence of oxen certainly makes it seem as though they intended to make a permanent home rather than a temporary trading center.

Even after the treaty in 1873, some of Routt County was still part of the Ute Reservation.[17] In 1878, Nathan Meeker accepted the post of agent

The Ute Trail, a pathway between the White River and Egeria Park, was traveled by the Utes on their seasonal passages through the Flattops. *Author's collection.*

for the Northern Utes. Meeker immediately started imposing his ideas on the Utes, as he had no tolerance for any way of life that differed from his. The more that Meeker persisted in his contention that the Utes use plows and barbed-wire fencing, the more the Indians defied him.[18] In the summer of 1879, the various Northern Ute bands left the agency contrary to Meeker's orders. They burned houses along the Yampa River and set fire to the surrounding forests. The final indignity for the Utes was when Meeker ordered their racetrack plowed up. At that time, Meeker lost any remaining respect and control of the Northern Utes.

Of the prominent Ute leaders, Colorow, Captain Jack and Douglass were among those who protested the most.[19] However, Meeker was not the only cause of the turmoil between the Utes and the encroaching settlers. The food, blankets and other provisions stored at the supply station in Rawlins, Wyoming, were not distributed to the Utes as had been promised.

The Indians were well armed and were joined by the more restless members of the Southern Utes. They went on a raid and killed settler Louis MacLean in eastern Colorado and also killed a man named Elliott in Middle Park. In spite of the unrest, Meeker refused to leave the reservation. Instead, he asked for military intervention. In response to this request,

Major Thornburg was dispatched from Fort Steele in Wyoming with three companies of cavalry and one company of infantry.

The Utes were watching the soldiers from the beginning. At Bear River (the Yampa River), Captain Jack and a few others entered the military camp and offered to guide the soldiers. They were refused, but Jack had accomplished his objective: he learned the strength of Thornburg's troops. The Utes ambushed the wagon train at Milk Creek, about twenty-five miles north of Nathan Meeker's headquarters. Almost all of the officers, except one lieutenant, were killed early in the battle. More than 150 mules were killed; this effectively immobilized the entire command. Both the soldiers and the Utes dug in for a prolonged siege.

Val FitzPatrick offered a different version of the Utes' motives. He maintained that Captain Jack and his friends were truly trying to warn the soldiers.[20] Jack wanted the whites to know that the White River Band could be pushed no more and would not allow the soldiers into the agency.

Early in the fight, Joe Rankin managed to leave the area undetected by the Utes. Thus, he was able to make his famous ride to Rawlins. He rode 160 miles in twenty-eight hours. A messenger had already been sent to Captain Dodge, who, with his company, was in Middle Park. He and his company of Buffalo Soldiers arrived at Milk Creek on the third day of the fight. These extra soldiers were not enough to stop the fight. It was not until the sixth day that General Merritt arrived from Wyoming with a large force.

About this same time, the warring Utes received a message from Chief Ouray of the Southern Utes asking them to stop fighting. Thirteen soldiers were killed, and forty-seven wounded. All twelve men at the Indian agency were killed. Mrs. Meeker, her daughter Josephine, Mrs. Price (wife of the blacksmith) and the Price's three-year-old daughter were kidnapped. Chief Douglas took them to his camp on the Grand River (Colorado River). Later, these captives were released at the urging of Chief Ouray and his wife, Chipeta. (The histories written at the time do not mention the losses that were sustained by the Utes.)

Those incidents, now called the Meeker Massacre, brought about a congressional inquiry. The result was an act of Congress that removed the Utes from Colorado to Utah in 1881. The move took about two weeks for the 1,400 Northern Utes. They started with about ten thousand sheep and goats and several thousand horses. By the time the Utes reached the reservation in Utah, many of their animals had died along the way.[21]

Many homesteaders and miners headed into the mountains and valleys of western Colorado, even before the last of the Uncompahgre Utes left in September 1881. Anglo-American settlers were laying out the towns of Grand Junction, Delta and Montrose on old Indian lands.[22]

Even though there were no town sites platted in South Routt County before the Utes left, a few people were in the area. In a letter written to the *Steamboat Pilot*, Billy Whipple mentioned that in 1879 several men wintered in the Egeria area. Those included Henry Crawford, Lafe Suits and his wife, Lewis Crouch, John Gibson, J.W. Whipple and Billy (Don Wilmer Whipple) himself.[23] These people started the winter living in Upper Egeria, perhaps Coberly Gulch. (This small, narrow valley extends up the west side of Spruce Divide east of Toponas.) As the winter progressed, they worked their way down Rock Creek toward the Grand River. In his note, Whipple added that James Ferguson and a "colored boy named Dave" spent the winter in Burns Hole.

In 1880, the following story was told by Z.B. Maudlin, an early cattleman in Axial Basin west of Craig:

I came here to the area on September 12, 1879; seventeen days later the Meeker Massacre occurred. At the time I was in Steamboat Springs, with my pal and partner Ed Hodges. The population of Steamboat consisted of four families. There were 22 men, 4 women and 10 or 12 children. We at once established a fortification, placed sentries and an outlook at night and prepared for an Indian attack. We later received a message from the Indians, themselves, "White people heap scared, Indian could kill all."[24]

In southern Routt County, early settlers' attitudes toward the Utes were influenced by such incidents as the following:

On our arrival in Florissant, father bought land and built a house (according to his notes, this would have been in 1874). The Ute Indians visited that country nearly every year on hunting trips. They were quite peaceable, and the settlers were accustomed to seeing them. Soon after our arrival at our new home, we children, playing outside the house, were startled to see a number of Indians sitting upon their ponies, looking down at us. The play ended abruptly when something like a stampede began. The door of the house was on the farthest side of the house. It is the habit of Indians when approaching a house, to divide their gang and surround it. Some of them had already reached the door when we reached it. To us there seemed nothing left to do but run for our lives, and that is what we did. On seeing the commotion, they were causing, one Indian tried to quiet us. He rode out from the group saying, "Ute no hurt. Ouray heap big chief." He spoke excellent English, and seemed much disturbed at having caused so much excitement. That party was Chief Ouray and his family. We saw many Indians in the years that followed. They were always friendly and very hungry.[25]

When David Gray's family settled in Lower Egeria, the Utes had already been relocated to Utah. However, rumors of impending attacks on the early settlers did occasionally happen. Gray had this to say:

After the settlement in 1883 no Indians were ever seen in Egeria Park, altho there was excitement at times of their approach. After 1887 or 1888, to the best of my memory, they came as far as the South Fork of the Williams River. [When looking at a map, this meant that the Utes were within an easy day's ride of Yampa, between fifteen and twenty miles, depending where they were on the South Fork.] *They were on a hunting trip, but as cattle were easier meat than wild game some slaughter was reported, also some horses were stolen. The settlers raised in arms and attacked them. After a spirited battle, the Indians were put to flight. They made a hasty retreat up the creek called Indian Run, thus the name. The Indians had some losses in men and horses and were never again seen on the north side of the White River Divide.*

Comments from other people who lived in the Yampa area were not as trusting as Gray's remarks seem to be. Other memories from the same period include: "My folks told of a conflict between Indians and whites in the real early days of settlement in what was then called Egeria Park. The Indians killed a white man without provocation and without warning. That was the attack on Elliott near Kremmling."[26] The Indians alleged some white man had killed a young "brave who had a squaw and two papooses," so Elliott was chosen because he had a wife and two children. This was the Indian version of "an eye for an eye and a tooth for a tooth."

Once while the men of the neighborhood were away working, word came to Mrs. [Rachel] *Crossan that the Indians were coming. She bundled her baby, Lila Egeria, up while her two boys and Myrtie* [the older daughter] *hitched the horses to the wagon, and they started off to warn the other women of the neighborhood. After going several miles they were able to return home, when it was proven to them that the "Indians" was only a lone Indian hunter!*[27]

A few short years after the Meeker Massacre, when everyone's nerves were on edge, someone came galloping into Yampa and shouted, "Indians have been sighted over on the burnt flats!"[28] As this was just a few miles west of the town of Yampa, there was a great commotion, and everyone grabbed their guns. They were ready for war. Some of the men rode to the burned flats to meet the Indians. When those fellows arrived, they found two of their own men. When everything was sorted out, it was discovered that the two men had been trying to slip up on a group of antelope. They had tied red bandannas on their hats while they crawled through the sagebrush and were mistaken for Utes.

It is likely this same scare gave rise to the following story. Since Ute hunting parties still came into the area during the summers, even though the U.S. government said they were to stay in Utah, many settlers felt that another massacre could happen. The major concern was that some of the younger Utes would attack and burn the outlying settlers' cabins. The following story was told by Tom Laughlin: Aunt Nan Roberts was a "strapping young woman" with bright red hair. Everyone kept teasing her by saying the Indians would enjoy having her hair for a scalp. One day, a rider came running in to the cabin yelling, "There are Indians out west on the Alkali Flats! I saw their feathers waving!" Aunt Nan grabbed the first thing she could find to cover her red hair. She did not want to give the Indians a chance to see that hair. The "cover up" was a dirty gray string mop.

Several of the men got together and rode west to meet the Indians. It was a false alarm. Two of the other settlers had tied red handkerchiefs to their hats. They had then been crawling through the sagebrush to slip close to a group of antelope. These two fellows were quite surprised when the rest of the men rode up and asked where the Indians were.

As might be expected, Nan never did live down her reaction to the "Indian raid." Her cousins continued to tell the story for years.

During the 1800s, northwestern Colorado, including Egeria Park, was well known and visited by many different people. The native peoples, the trappers and explorers, the gold seekers and the inquisitive travelers all found the area. Some of them may not have left written records, but the clues to their past give fascinating material for our speculation.

2

FIRST HOMESTEADERS

B efore the government officially opened the area to settlement, many people predicted the opening of homestead land in western Colorado. Prior to the Meeker Massacre in 1879, countless trappers and adventurers traveled through Egeria Park. Some of these people were looking for land for their families and friends. By the time the Utes left Colorado, rumors of the beautiful parks had started to circulate; those reports were a major influence on families' decisions to locate here.

There are discrepancies in the documentation of who came into Egeria during the 1880s. The inconsistency of those dates is due to several factors. Much of the history was kept orally by individual families and not recorded until several years after the events occurred.

Some of the first homesteaders did not file their claims at the land office for a year or more after they had built their cabins because of the great distance between Egeria Park and the land office in Idaho Springs. This was more than one hundred miles and over two mountain passes: Gore Pass and Berthoud Pass. Later, they had to travel to Glenwood Springs; this was an easier trip, but still more than ninety miles with inadequate roads and trails.

Others would settle for a year or two then sell their cabins and other improvements before they officially owned the land. The new settler would claim the original inhabitant's time and improvements as part of the requirements needed by the government to own the land.

Occasionally, when looking back, the old-timers couldn't remember for sure when an event occurred. Because they desired to be remembered as "original pioneers," they would date that episode at the earliest possible time.

Dave Gray (grandson of David and Mary (Bird) Gray) noted, "As no records were kept, it is difficult and, in some cases, impossible to be accurate. This is especially true in giving dates."[29] Some of the children of those first homesteaders wrote articles, manuscripts or books about those early years in Egeria Park. Dates are only as accurate as the original writers could make them. Many of the early settlers are listed here, but this is certainly not a complete record of everyone who lived in Egeria at that time.

In 1879, several people stayed in Egeria Park and in the McCoy area, including Henry Crawford, James Ferguson, Lafe Suits and his wife, Lewis Crouch, John S. Gibson, J.W. Whipple, D.W. Whipple, Dave Baker, Henry Wright and a black man named Dave, who stayed with James Ferguson.[30] Some of these pioneers started the winter in Coberly Gulch, east of what is now Toponas. Then they moved on down toward the mouth of Rock Creek near the Grand River, which is now the Colorado River.

In 1880, Peter Simon, Lou Wilson, Sam Fix and John Sprunk came into the valley.[31] This could also have been the year that William Bird, his son Albert and a sheriff by the name of Watson followed a stolen team into the valley.

The entire Bird family was in the valley and well established by 1883, as Ed Smith of Hayden reminisced that fifty years before he was "always welcome when he was driving cattle thru."[32] This statement would indicate that Albert, Tom and Lewis Bird came into the valley in 1881 with the family following in 1882; otherwise, the various Bird families would not have been well established by 1883.

The William Montgomery family came in 1881. (The Montgomery records give the date as 1882.) The Arnold family arrived in 1882. The VanCamps acquired homestead rights from Joe Ward in 1883. Between 1882 and 1883, Egeria settlers included William Bird, Albert Bird, Tom Nickels, Elmer Hoag, Ed Watson, L. Garbarino, Jim Scott, L.L. Wilson, Riley Wilson and John Phillips.[33]

A Mrs. Watson was the only woman to spend the winter of 1882.[34] The spring of 1883 brought the wives of the homesteaders mentioned before as well as more families: Alex Gray, Will King, Sam Tharp, Herod Fulton, Mark Choate, Tom Gibbs, Leo Thayer, John R. Brown, Billy Rockhill, Elmer Hoag and "Auntie" Hoag.[35]

Many of the people who migrated into the Lower Egeria area between 1880 and 1885 were related. The William and Mary Ellen (Wilson) Bird family was quite large. They had ten children; six or seven remained in the area. The eleven children in the Robert and Jane (Wilson) Bird family were

The Arnold house on Moffat Avenue, 2006. *Author's collection.*

older. Those cousins arrived in the Yampa area in the mid-1880s. Lawson, Omler and Riley Bird settled in the Egeria Park area, as did their sister Frances, who was married to Robert Laughlin. (Robert Laughlin bought the rights to the Watson homestead in 1885.) Willis Bird lived in Colburn but came to Yampa quite often to visit. No wonder this area was called "Bird Haven."[36]

Some of the other relatives arriving in Egeria Park at that time include Lewis L. Wilson (his mother was a Bird) and Mary Bird (William and Robert Bird's sister), who was married to Alex Gray. Margaret Bird married Tom Gibbs. Parille Bird was married to Mark Choate. Elizabeth Wilson was married to John Phillips.

These families lived in Missouri just before and during the Civil War. After the war, they were trying to find somewhere to bring their families for jobs and land. Some of them established a home near Florissant, Colorado; others settled just east of Colorado Springs. They must have communicated regularly, as they certainly all seemed willing to move to the Yampa Valley during a five-to-six-year span in the 1880s.

After proving up their homesteads and selling them to others, both Lawson Bird and Omler Bird moved back to Missouri.

Some of the first homesteaders that came into Upper Egeria were in Breckenridge before they moved into Routt County. In her book *Mother*

24

The Robert Laughlin's ranch, circa 1890. *Herold family collection.*

Remembers, May (King) Wilson wrote of coming to Egeria Park: "There were about half a dozen men who went to what is now Toponas, Colorado. They all settled on Egeria Creek and King Creek....My father [Preston King] made a number of trips to make surveys."[37] Preston King and his wife, Mary, settled on what became known as King Creek. Wilson related that her uncle Will Reed, her friend Myrtie Crossan (Macfarlane), Myrtie's parents (George and Rachel Crossan) and Agnes Mandall, a hired girl, all went to their homesteads in November 1884. She placed the Crowners "about six miles down the country" at that time and stated that those were the only people in Upper Egeria that winter.

The next spring, the S.D. Wilson, the Sam Reed and the "Cap" Newcomer families all moved to the area. Ed Macfarlane had a ranch. "Mr. Sutton who had a sawmill in Breckenridge took up a ranch down the creek from us and lived on it two winters"[38] Miss Nash came to Upper Egeria to teach school in 1885. In the spring of 1886, Captain Tibbets came from Burns Hole to teach school. These were both summer schools, as they concluded by the first of August so the children could help with the haying.

Wilson mentioned that in 1888, Anna Williams married a trapper named Frank Smith. They lived at the head of the fork on Egeria Creek. Frank's brother Tom Smith evidently worked with them in running an elk ranch. "Uncle" Charlie Morris was one of King's neighboring ranchers. Wilson

Preston and Mary Adella King, circa 1890. *Courtesy of Yampa-Egeria Museum.*

also mentioned a "Mrs. Smith who lived up on the head of Egeria Creek, right under the Flat Tops." (Perhaps this is the same Anna Williams who married Frank Smith.)

In his manuscript, Dave Gray listed the people he thought were in the area between 1884 and 1890. Beginning in Upper Egeria, there were Tony and Phil Sterner, Ed and Jim Macfarlane, Charley Morris, Bill Crowner, Kate Morse, Bert Acton, the Lafon family, the Charles and Arthur Leighton families and Albert Colby. There was the John Sumner family, the Arnold Powell family, Jim and Bill Laramore's families, Herb Moore, Jack Hill, Willis Bird, John Minor, Omler Bird and family, John Lees, the Douglas Lees family and Belle McBride. Most of these people settled in Lower Egeria.

In the Arnold family, there were Mr. and Mrs. Arnold and their children: Bill, Charlie, Maggie, Harry, George, Frank and Fred. Dora G. Wilson (Mrs. L.L. Wilson) arrived about the same time. Frank Groh, Tom and Fritz Wohler and George Stafford (who married Mrs. Henry Crawford) arrived in the valley prior to 1890.

Top: Trapping was a source of income for the early settlers. The Clark LaFons in Upper Egeria. *Courtesy of Yampa-Egeria Museum; photo by Clark Lafon.*

Bottom: H.E. and Bertha Moore's house, June 1928. *Herold family collection.*

The Franz and Dave Chapman families, Martin Tschudi and wife, Emma Walker, Anna Bowen, Cora Bowen, Ben and Bill Male, Mike Cox, the Jim Cox family, William and Ross Henny, Newt and Ira Mounts, William Thayer and family, Mart Boor and the William Boor family all arrived during those years, as did others.

Margaret Crawford, with Margaret Chapman driving, circa 1925. *Courtesy of Yampa-Egeria Museum.*

Van Camp Cabins, once the home of the infamous Joe Ward, pictured here around 1980. *Herold family collection.*

In 1886, Henry Hernage started a store where Yampa is now located. In the same year, William Montgomery settled nearby. In 1884, the Ward family had been replaced by VanCamp.

Of the early settlers on Bear River above Yampa, the following list was furnished by Ruby Neiman (daughter of W.W. Carle). Elijah Moody came in 1884. Nicholas Mandall and family came in 1885. A.C. Burgess arrived at about the same time. Morris Lancaster, his father, Jim and Paul Elgin and W.W. Carle and family came in 1888.

In 1889, the Buttricks, the Bijous, Lem Lindsey, T.P. Lindsey and his wife (Auntie) migrated to Egeria. Isaac Bijou was Annie (also called "Auntie") Buttrick's father, and Auntie and Minnie Bijou were sisters.

The Hoskinsons and Hutchinsons came in 1889. They and the Mandalls, Lancasters, Elgins, Carles and A.C. Burgess were from Summit County.

Those people who arrived in the valley in the early 1880s faced extreme isolation and winter hardships. Stories throughout this book relate tales of these incidents, but the following gives some insight into those first winters.

Ruby (Carle) Neiman, circa 1890. *Yampa-Egeria Museum, Fogg Collection.*

Minnie (Bejou) Lindsey, circa 1885.
Yampa-Egeria Museum, Fogg Collection.

Meat was no problem, for there were deer and elk in abundance.[39] In 1882, the first heavy snow came in early October. With the exception of spots on southern hillsides, that snow stayed until the next spring. That winter became known to be the hardest winter for those early settlers.

These new arrivals had never purchased provisions for so long a period of time, and everybody ran out of something, usually necessities. Exchanges were made as far as possible. By April, lard and cooking fat stores were so low as to be practically nonexistent.

That winter, two trappers, Al Martin and Jim Benett, were living in the Oak Creek Basin about two miles north of the site of the town of Oak Creek. Two other trappers, Tom Smith and Hank Veach, were on Trout Creek where Ben Male later homesteaded.

One morning about April 20, Tom Smith followed his trap line up Trout Creek. Far up on a mountain side he noticed a fresh breaking of snow, which seemed to indicate that some hibernating animal had roused from slumber and tunneled out to look for spring. Upon investigation, he discovered that a grizzly bear had come out, found the snow too soft for traveling and returned to the den.

Being a man of great courage, Smith looked into the tunnel. He found it to be very deep, 20 or more feet under the drift, and quite dark at the bottom. The opening was large, so he ventured inside. Before he had gone far, he heard a deep growl. At the same time, he noticed the white of teeth near at hand. After aiming a careful shot at the teeth, he started hastily out of the tunnel with the bear at his heels.

Luckily, the snow would hold up the weight of the man but not that of the bear. As soon as Smith had time to reload his gun, he killed the bear. The first shot, fired at the bear's teeth, had struck a tusk, which deflected the bullet so that it had simply cut the bear's lip.

This bear, according to Dave Gray, was the largest ever killed in this part of the country. There was no method of weighing it, however, so its bulk was just estimated. Those who knew something of the weight of animals thought it about 1,200 pounds. When the skin was off, the fat was found to be about four inches thick over the entire body.

The trappers cut the fat into strips, loaded it on trail sleds and hauled the bounty to Egeria, where it found a ready sale at ten cents a pound. This greatly relieved the fat situation, furnishing the settlers with a "fine oil, tho it was better suited to oiling harness than baking biscuits."

It is worth repeating that David Gray was a boy when he came into the Yampa Valley. He wrote the article with the preceding story and published it in the *Steamboat Pilot* some sixty years after he arrived in Egeria Park.

Those mentioned seem to make a reasonable list of the early settlers, but the dates are not automatically correct. Trying to establish a date of arrival for the early pioneers is more difficult than relating the fact that people were residents. The discrepancy in dates reflects the differences of the various sources.

This is certainly not meant to be a total list of the people who came into the valley in the 1880s, but it demonstrates that numerous people came in at that time and settled throughout both Upper and Lower Egeria Park. The goal is to start a list of those early settlers so that others can add to it. It is impressive that the early settlers not only knew one another but also visited back and forth regularly, even though it was a large geographic area with primitive transportation.

3

FREIGHT WAGONS, STAGECOACHES AND RAILROADS

Northwestern Colorado has been called the "Last Frontier," "The Land of the Last Pioneers" and the "Place That Time Forgot." These poetic names all refer to the fact that Routt County was among the last places in the continental United States to be settled. (Moffat County and Routt County were not divided into two counties until 1911.) When one looks at a physical map of Colorado, one can see the reason for this anomaly. The high mountains surround the valley on three sides. The fourth side, to the north, faced Wyoming Territory with its great distances to any town of large size. The people who traveled the transcontinental trails to the north were trying to go to Oregon or Utah. The miners that ascended into the mountains on the east side of the valley were looking for gold or silver. They were not looking for a permanent place to settle. This meant that roads were not built into the area until after the Utes left in 1881.

Even after the first rudimentary roads were built, stagecoaches and wagons occasionally had accidents. When autos started becoming popular, roads had to be even better to accommodate the faster speeds. The railroad companies also found that the area was a challenge. Gore Canyon was an incredibly difficult terrain in which to lay tracks. Another obstacle for the railroad was getting loaded trains up the long climb between Phippsburg and Toponas. The trains had to have helper engines to make that steep grade. Today, the railroad still has to place extra engines on the coal trains to climb out of the valley.

Game trails, horse tracks and Ute paths were the avenues into the valley when the first white settlers arrived. When Sir George Lord Gore visited the valley in 1854, he and his accompanying retinue did not bring their wagons over the pass, which is now named Gore Pass in Sir George's honor. The trails used by bands of Arapahoe and Utes were steep and narrow. It was these trails that the homesteaders widened and eventually surveyed that became present-day roads into Egeria Park.

The roads into the valley were exhausting and demanding at best and at times quite hazardous. Almost every person to write about travel to Egeria Park in those first few years mentioned problems with the roads. James Crawford had this comment on the lack of roads in 1874 when he tried to follow the river into the Steamboat Springs area: "So rough was this canyon that they could not haul the cart through it. Jimmy and Hute decided to continue afoot up the stream....Next morning they struck another canyon and had a very tedious time going through it."[40]

Ten years later, Mary King had this to say about the road on Gore Pass.

I was pretty nearly scared to death. Just two ruts made a road. Once in a while there was a place where you could turn out and go by. Leaving one gulch, we would go up another gulch, and down, and around a hill, and up another gulch. Some places were pretty steep, and the road was narrow....It was November and ice had begun to form and the creek had overflowed.... We caught up with the freighters; they had struck that hill and were stuck. What the men had to do was to unhitch the four-horse teams and make a string of teams that was long enough to reach up the hill, where the leaders could get a foothold in the snow. I don't know how many horses they had to put on to get up there, but they put on team after team and drove on up the hill....We had crossed the Range and were going down on the other side when we had to go through a place called the Devil's Dive, almost straight down one side and the straight up the other....Later on, my father surveyed the road that went up the canyon, instead of going over the hill, and they had a good grade. But in those early days people hadn't built any roads. They just followed a trail.[41]

Dave Gray stated that Sam Tharp was elected as county commissioner in 1886.[42] His efforts established the county road through Egeria Park. "Preston King was the surveyor, Sam Tharp, Milton Woolery and William Bird were viewers and plowmen, and he (Dave Gray) was the chain carrier."

Horse-drawn road grader. *Herold family collection.*

Even after it was surveyed, it took time for the road to be leveled and improved. That first road through the valley followed the sagebrush hills down the center of the area. Some of the original road can be seen in various pastures throughout the valley. The present highway follows the railroad tracks rather than the pioneer road.

Even though the first roads tried to follow the hillsides rather than go through the lowest part of the valley, there were wet areas that the roads occasionally had to cross. The pioneer answer to that was to corduroy the wet spots. This meant that logs or poles were placed transversely across the road over the mud holes. There are still places in the existing county roads where one can find the corduroy logs under the gravel.

Francis Moore said that in the early days of Routt County, Albert Bird was contracted to build a road, suitable for freight wagons.[43] It was to leave the Gore Pass road at Toponas and go south twenty-five miles to the Routt County line, just a couple hundred yards from the town of McCoy. This was to be a complete road with bridges, culverts and all for $600. There was no survey for this road, so Albert did not pay any attention to steep grades; if he came to a hill, he just went up and over it—more or less in the shortest way.

Later, in 1905, the *Yampa Leader* had this note about Albert: "Albert Bird has been appointed road commissioner for the Yampa district by the county commissioners."[44]

Top: Hand labor on the rock abutment for a bridge. *Herold family collection.*

Bottom: The first touring car to visit the Antlers Hotel in Yampa, 1907. *Herold family collection.*

In 1913, instead of attempting to travel over the high passes of Berthoud and Gore, Gus Bower (a well-known Yampa businessman) traveled from Denver to Fort Collins, Tie Siding, Rawlins, Baggs and Craig to get to Yampa.[45] He spent four days on this 452-mile journey with his new Apperson

Jack Rabbit automobile. Gus's wife, returning from California, met him in Denver but traveled to Yampa by railroad rather than undertake the arduous trip in the new car.

Automobiles had to have better roads that were less steep than those traveled by wagons. As people acquired more cars, they wanted more and better-quality roads. Cars were jacked up (to help preserve their tires) and stored in barns during the winter because the roads were not plowed and were not kept open after the first few snows. Besides, there was no antifreeze for the radiators when it was cold; the radiators had to be drained to prevent freezing when they were not in use. During the 1920s, it became a matter of pride to see who had the bragging rights for the last trip from Yampa to Steamboat Springs before it snowed up entirely. Wintertime travel was still demanding and depended on horses, sleds or the ever-popular skis.

When the first settlers came into the valley, their best and most economical source of supplies was Denver. There were towns at Empire, Leadville, Georgetown, Breckenridge and so on, but the mining frenzy guaranteed inflated prices for any provisions bought in those towns. Getting stores from Denver was a two-week trip with heavy wagons. Of course, if there was bad weather, road problems or wagon breakdowns it would take even more time.

Four-horse team pulling Yampa's first gasoline wagon. The teamster, Elmer Margerum, delivered gasoline from McCoy to Oak Creek. *Herold family collection.*

By the 1920s, Model T Fords were a common sight in Yampa. *Herold family collection.*

During the early 1880s, many wagonloads of wild game, both elk and venison, went from Egeria Park to different mining towns as trade for supplies or cash.[46] Breckenridge, Leadville, Empire and Georgetown all had markets for meat. Stolen beef was sold in these towns as easily as wild game.

Those early settlers were a long way from their source of supplies.[47] Before he was married, Herb Moore did a large amount of freighting not only for himself but also for others in the area when he first came into the valley. He brought in many loads for the Hernage store as well as for individual settlers. Even though it took two or three days longer, Moore usually made Denver his main source. Most people tried to make a limit of two trips a year: one in the spring and one in the fall. Moore said it was never a problem to make up another load; someone always needed something. For several years, Denver was the nearest railway.

Herb Moore told of one skittish young team he had broken just prior to a supply run. By the time he got to Denver, they were getting tender feet, so he took them to a blacksmith and told him, "They might be hard to manage, as they have never been shod." Everything was so new and strange to that team that they just stood quietly and trembled without giving the blacksmith a bit of trouble.

Moore was certainly not the only one to ferry supplies into the area. Both the Birds and the Wilsons hauled freight into the area, and undoubtedly there were others. If the homesteaders had an extra team or two, they would go in the fall to get their own supplies and would bring in other people's supplies as well. This was one way to make a little extra money. Because of the two high passes, Berthoud Pass and Gore Pass, the freighting season was rather short. It was a piece of good fortune to the people of this whole valley when the railway built down the Eagle River to make Wolcott a much nearer source of goods.

The railroad from Denver to Wolcott was built almost twenty years before Moffat laid the tracks into the Yampa Valley. After Wolcott had a railroad but before Routt County did, the fastest and closest way to get into the valley from Denver was by train to Wolcott. Both passengers and mail traveled this route. For a short time, one stage ran from Wolcott to Yampa; a different line ran to Steamboat Springs, with a third line continuing on to Hayden. Before long, a route from Wolcott to Steamboat Springs was established, with branch lines going from there to Hahn's Peak, the county seat at that time, or to Hayden and Craig. After it became one stage route, the stage ran from Wolcott to Steamboat Springs one day, then went from Steamboat Springs back to Wolcott the next day—without an overnight stop. One direction for this trip was sixteen hours or more depending upon the weather. Soon, the stages ran every day. Since Yampa was considered the halfway stop, the passengers spent the night in the Antlers Hotel.

It was said that one of the drivers never went to bed. He just went to a saloon, where he sat in a chair in the corner and tipped his black hat down over his face. Evidently, he could doze and sleep that way, as he was always ready to go on to Steamboat Springs the next day.

For several years starting in 1888, two brothers, J.W. Whipple and Don Wilmer "Billy" Whipple, ran the stage line from Wolcott to Steamboat. Billy Whipple ran the stage for more than twenty-one years with various partners; the *Pilot* listed F.E. Milner, W.C. Shaw, Milby Frazier and P.F. Reinhardt.[48] Billy Whipple not only had part interest in the stage line, but he also acted as the stage driver at different times throughout the years.

A.J. Stafford, an early partner of Billy Whipple's, was killed when driving the stage in September 1888. This occurred on the Riley Wilson Hill about a quarter of a mile north of Phippsburg during a runaway.[49] The passengers all escaped with nothing more than minor injuries.

Several different houses and locations claim to be stage stops between Wolcott and Steamboat Springs. It is possible that many of these homes could have been stage stops at different times. The drivers not only had to change horses occasionally but also stopped for meals at different locations.

Wolcott to Steamboat Springs stage, circa 1908. *Herold family collection.*

The stages stopped at the homes where the women were good cooks and willing to feed a coach full of people. At different points of time, the stage through Egeria Park stopped at such places as the William Montgomery home (half a mile south of Yampa) and the VanCamp house (the first cabin built in Yampa), but the most famous was the Antlers Hotel in Yampa.

As the stage traveled on down the valley, the "Diamond Window" cabin and the Inn on top of Yellow Jacket Divide were both stops, as were various houses in the town of Sidney.

Another stage line ran from Kremmling over Gore Pass into Upper Egeria then on into Yampa. This line lasted until about the time that the Moffat Railroad reached Egeria Park in 1908. One of the stage stops for this line was a large two-story log building built by the Gates family. That building is currently in the National Register of Historic Places and can be seen off Gore Pass on U.S. Forest Service Road 206.

The railroad had a great influence on Egeria Park before it arrived, as well as after it finally reached the valley. The anticipation and excitement of opening up the valley to larger settlement inspired the interest of many speculators. Many of those investors believed in the area and made their permanent homes here. The railroad opened up the valley for easier access to the outside and a way to ship the farming and ranching products from the area. It also facilitated access to the large coal fields throughout the entire Yampa Valley, including the towns of Oak Creek, Haybro and Mount Harris. The company towns of Haybro and Mount Harris did not survive the closing of the coal mines, but Oak Creek is still a viable town. The influence of the railroad affected the entire northwestern corner of the state.

The survey for the railroad came through the valley in 1903. Entrepreneurs and businessmen from Denver, New York and even England were interested in the "Empire of Routt County."[50] Judge Morning mentioned, "During the year 1903 about forty buildings, all good substantial ones, were built in Yampa, involving an expenditure of over $40,000." This building boom brought in many new businesses.

In the summer of 1905, Sam Nay and his brother Will contracted to furnish the meat for the Moffat Railroad crews.[51] At the beginning of the contract, the railroad had reached as far as Hot Sulfur Springs; the Nays furnished all the meat to the crews until the railroad reached Steamboat Springs in December 1908. By June 1906, Sam was slaughtering and delivering about ten head of beef each week to the different crews. At that time, Sam's slaughterhouse was in Kremmling.

In April 1907, Sam leased the Gibbs ranch (near Finger Rock about two miles south of Yampa). The need for meat had more than doubled, so the Yampa area became his headquarters. He continued furnishing meat for the railroad as the track was laid between McCoy and Steamboat Springs.

During the summer of 1908, everyone in the valley seemed to be anticipating the arrival of the Moffat Railroad. The following news clips were found in the *Yampa Leader*:

At the Crowner ranch, five miles south of Yampa and midway between this town and Toponas, a sidetrack has been put in, which will be known as Trapper's Siding. This side track is 3000 feet long and will give ample facilities for passing when the heavy traffic resulting from the Oak Creek coal fields has been established.[52]

It is expected that with the opening of the road to Yampa, the mail will immediately be ordered brought to this point on the railway mail car, to be distributed from here to the different post offices in Routt county. This will bring Yampa within 10 hours of Denver by mail, while now, with the mail being delivered to the railroad at McCoy, it requires 29½ hours for a letter

Engine for the Edna Mine Company. *Yampa-Egeria Museum, Fogg Collection.*

to travel from Yampa to Denver. The Denver morning papers will reach here
the same day they are published, the mail being distributed at the post office
here that evening.[53]

The first passenger train arrived in Yampa on September 9, 1908.
"About 70 passengers from Denver alighted from the train."[54] Many of these
passengers were the elected officials of the county. The train consisted of the
engine, a mail and baggage car, two passenger coaches and D.H. Moffat's
private car, the *Marcia*. (This car is now exhibited in Craig and can be toured
there.) Moffat, S.M. Perry, their families and guests were all traveling to the
Perry Coal Mine in Oak Creek for an inspection tour.

The Town of Yampa turned down the opportunity to host the roundhouse
and railroad yards. The Moffat Railroad then bought the homestead that had
been Alex Gray's from Lewis Wilson. That area then became the bustling
railroad town of Phippsburg. The town housed not only railroad workers
but also some of the miners that lived in nearby towns.

Toponas, Yampa and Phippsburg all had sidings where railroad cars
could be positioned for loading. Next to the sidings, corrals with loading
chutes were built so livestock could easily be loaded into the railroad
cars. Many cars of cattle and sheep were sent during the next fifty years.
Before the tracks reached Hayden and Craig (the railroad did not reach
Hayden until December 1912 and Craig in 1913),[55] cattle and sheep from

The Alex Gray homestead, trains and water tank at the Phippsburg railroad yards, circa 1910. *Yampa-Egeria Museum, Fogg Collection.*

Engine in the Phippsburg railroad yards, unidentified oiler. *Courtesy of Karen Craig.*

those areas were shipped from Phippsburg, Yampa and a little later from Steamboat Springs.

When livestock was shipped on the railroad, someone representing the owners almost always rode in the caboose of the train. When the train stopped to load water into the steam engines at the various stations, the cowboys would check the cattle cars and prod any animals that were lying down to get them on their feet so they wouldn't get trampled.

Those sidings and others built up and down the valley were also used for both the lettuce and the lumber industries. Potatoes were also shipped from the area. Two of the more interesting items sent by rail were milk and cream. The farmers and homesteaders sent full milk and cream cans to both Steamboat Springs and Denver from about 1910 through the 1950s. The empty cans were then returned to the ranchers on the next train.

Even though many other products were sent by rail, coal was the major catalyst for building the railroad.

While the railroad was an improvement over other forms of transportation, it was not always an enjoyable trip. As late as the 1930s, there were some problems. Tirzah Hamidy offered her impressions in 1931.

Steam engine stopping at the Yampa depot. *Herold family collection.*

We are still going through the tunnel. This is the blackest, longest tunnel of all and the trainmen have closed all the ventilators and going around to see that a window isn't opened—gas, I guess. It seems to be seeping in somewhere and the train is just sort of clouding and sickening hot. The gas is getting worse, I believe, and we are still going through the tunnel. What a road this is....It's about three now and I'm getting so tired and never felt so dirty. My suit is quite warm—a little too warm. Hate to put my coat back on. We're going through Yampa now. I just washed and powdered my nose to be sure and be ready for Oak Creek. We don't get there for just one hour.[56]

Even after living in Oak Creek for many years, Hamidy felt that her original train ride into the Yampa Valley was very challenging:

Mike Yurich, a former student and a good friend, has asked me to write a few lines giving my impression of Oak Creek when I first arrived....I came by train and after going through the tunnels my clothes were covered with soot from the steam engine, my hands and face were dirty, I was tired and hungry and there was no one to meet me. I sat and waited in the dreary little station for nearly an hour while the person who was to meet me was "out fishing." If there had been another train back to Denver that day, I would have been on it.[57]

Tirzah Hamidy's husband related that she was a schoolteacher.[58] Before their marriage, she worked at the *Denver Post*, under Major Bonfils. She was his private secretary before she came up to the Yampa Valley to teach school.

⊙━✦━⊙

The tools that different people used in different professions were those of personal preference; the cowboys, freighters and stage drivers were no exception. The cowboys that came from West Texas and New Mexico used ropes when working with cattle. The rawhide riata was a product of Spanish influence. The manila rope was made of twisted plant fibers. It evolved into modern synthetic ropes made of nylon.

Today's rodeo cowboys use a different type for every kind of roping, one stiffness to rope the head, then another stiffness to rope the heels. Modern ranchers use more of an all-purpose nylon rope. But even in the early days of the country, individuals had their own preference. Some cowboys obtained rawhide ropes; a few people in the area even made their own. The early cowboys and ranchers favored the manila-type rope. Each cowboy had a length he preferred; the cowboys who rode on the Great Plains used a much longer rope than those who worked in the thick brush of Texas. Most of the stockmen in this area had thirty to thirty-five feet of rope coiled on their saddles.

A few people preferred a bullwhip when working stock. Some stockmen used both the whip and a rope. Bill Gardner grew up helping in the stage station at Yellow Jacket Pass; he began working there when he was twelve or thirteen years old.[59] Bill learned to use the longer bullwhips when he worked with the four-horse and six-horse teams. Amazingly enough, Bill could flick a fly off a lead horse's ear without interrupting the team's progress. Bill's use of the bullwhip was truly unique; he could control it equally well with either hand.

After Bill was older and owned a ranch (about five miles northeast of Phippsburg, on Thorpe Mountain), he always carried a whip coiled on one side of his saddle and a rope on the other side. Bill had every horse he owned trained so he could ride the horse and use the whip. His horse would run alongside of the hindquarters of a cow so Bill could then use the whip to turn the animal in either direction.

Other people used a bullwhip instead of a rope when working cattle; it depended on what was to be accomplished. At one time, Herb Moore bragged on his ability in using a bullwhip, or black snake, as they are sometimes called.[60] Herb said as a kid while helping his father in timber work, they used oxen exclusively. He came to be an expert with a bullwhip and could cut a fly off an ox's back and never touch a hair. Perhaps he stretched that a little; however, Francis Moore did see him use a bullwhip one time to great advantage.

When Francis was a boy about ten years old, Herb and Francis went down to Guilliam's place to get a bull and bring him home. (This would have been about 1919.) Guilliam lived just outside Oak Creek at the railroad crossing south of town. They started out but had gone less than a mile when the bull decided to go back. Francis got right in front of him with his horse but that bull just pushed past Francis and was on his way home. Herb moved in front of him and cut him right between the eyes with his bullwhip. It peeled a streak of hair from the hide about two inches long. The bull not only stopped but also turned around and drove just like an old milk cow all the way to Yampa. If Herb had not had the bullwhip and knew how to use it, Francis was certain the bull would have given them much trouble. Of course, this was long before the days of trucks and stock trailers—today it would be much easier to travel that ten miles.

A saddle was another item through which early residents showed their individuality. The townspeople and the occasional rider either owned or rented a "standard saddle." Most of the saddles in this area had high cantles and horns. The cowboys, bronc riders and horse breakers all had their own ideas of what a saddle should be. A few of the bronc riders even rode a full bull moose or half moose saddle, with the pommels extending out over the rider's legs so it was more difficult to fall out of the saddle. Almost all the older saddles had a shorter seat than our western saddles of today. Some early riders dallied their rope to the saddle horn; others believed in tying the end of the rope to the saddle horn. Before 1910, most women rode sidesaddle, although a few wore split skirts or even borrowed their husbands' pants and rode astride when they were not in town. By the 1920s, almost all the women in this area rode astride.

The perseverance of those early settlers was truly incredible in building the roads and the railroad. In all of northwestern Colorado, including Egeria Park, evidence of those early roads can still be seen today. The Utes, the trappers, the teamsters, the stage drivers, the train engineers and even the domestic livestock all followed the paths first established by the movement of wild animals.

4

HAY, GRAIN AND OTHER CROPS

Clearing the land of brush, trees or willows is the first requirement for planting new ground with a crop. When the homesteaders first came into the valley, much of the land was covered with cottonwood trees that followed the course of the river. The willows spread back and forth along the rest of the bottomland. Small pockets of grass were found in the midst of those willows. There were several distinct species of willows, the larger trunked "tree" willow as well as the slenderer bush willows. When the willows were cleared, sedges and grasses quickly took over the ground. Those were the meadows the homesteaders cut to make hay for their animals. The higher ground, where the sagebrush, sarvis berries and oak brush grew, was cleared for small grains and other crops. The uncleared land was considered open range for cattle during the summer months. Each year, homesteaders were able to clear more land to use for cropland. The bottomland was cleared and used for wild hay, or meadow hay; the brush-covered hillsides were cleared for grain and alfalfa fields.

H.E. "Herb" Moore came into the county about four years after the Birds.[61] He asked Tom Nickels (who lived on the homestead just east of Grandpa Bird's) if Nickels had any work for him. Nickels asked Moore if he wore gloves. Moore replied that he used them to protect his hands when he worked. Nickels said that the kids he knew put on gloves but did not really do any work. Nickels did give Moore a chance to prove himself.

Nickels asked, "Do you see all those willows?" pointing to meadows on the forty acres directly north of Yampa. "Those all need chopped out."

Herb Moore made a deal with Tom Nickels to cut the shrubs and bushes. Nickels then went to Denver for some reason. At that time, people estimated that it would take about two weeks for the trip to Denver and back. Moore had learned to use an axe in Texas cutting hickory and other hardwoods, so he thought it was "almost fun" to chop on the willows. He said that one good swing of the axe would cut about halfway through the trunk of one of the tree willows that covered the valley at that time.

When Nickels got back from Denver, he found Moore in the pool hall. He asked Moore how he was getting along with the willows. Herb Moore replied that he was through cutting them all out. Nickels did not believe him, so Moore simply told him to go and look.

"It is amazing to think of the struggle it must have been for the pioneers in this Egeria Park area to get a foothold; for them to clear enough land and at the same time raise enough food for themselves and their livestock."[62]

Clearing willows from meadowland was slow work. To find enough ground to cut for hay, Robert Laughlin would take his "cradle," as it was called, and move through any small openings in the willows hunting more grass. (A cradle was a long-bladed scythe. It had several upright fingers attached so that when the scythe was swung in a long arc, it carried the cut grass with it to the end of the swing. This left a neat row of cut grass as the

Francis Moore's "gas twenty" with a grain drill, 1930. *Herold family collection.*

mower advanced each step.) While the Laughlin "boys" used horses to mow and stack the hay in the areas already cleared of willows, Robert constantly moved in the willows with his cradle, hunting more grass. That scythe hung high in the barn loft for many years.

The Laughlin boys—Walter, Ben and Tom—all helped with the hay from a very young age. To clear those small plots of ground in the first few years, they gathered the cut, dried hay and piled it onto old cowhides. A rope was attached to one corner of the cowhide, and the other end was wrapped around a saddle horn so they could pull the hay into the main stack. They also employed this method of moving hay for some of their neighbors. At times, two boys worked together, each with a saddle horse and a rope tied to an adjoining corner of the hide. They would then race back to the barn or stack with that load of hay. No wonder they were all good riders and horse trainers as they got older.

In 1928 or 1929, Francis Moore used his first crawler tractor, a gas 20 Caterpillar, or clearing willows to make meadows for Henry Knott on what was called the Stafford family's homestead.[63] This is just north of the larger Laughlin Buttes. Francis said the willows cut off easily with the cat. It was in the spring of the year, and the ground had thawed for just the top two inches. He was able to shear the willows off right at the ground.

Herb Moore told of one spring when the Laughlins ran out of hay and there was still quite a bit of snow everywhere in early March. None of the neighbors had any hay to spare either. For that reason, Robert Laughlin and his sons took horses and broke a trail in the snow on Greenridge, up Lawson Creek, to those steep hillsides that face the south sun, where the snow was beginning to melt. They moved their cattle up there, and the animals were able to find grass under the brush and survive until spring. This may have been the same year (about 1885 or 1886) that some of the Bird families had to move their cattle down to the Burns Hole area during the winter.

The following information appeared in an October 1905 *Yampa Leader*: "W.D. Jones, living about four miles west of Yampa left a sample of the first cutting of his alfalfa, which was cut August 13, and measuring from where the mower cut it off was 4 feet: 3 inches tall and had a heavy foliage."[64] Why did he wait until October to bring in hay that had been cut in August? Was this the first time he had gone to town since he cut the hay in August? Whatever the reason, it sounds like good hay.

For several years, Francis Moore contracted to stack hay for Kenneth Hawkins as well as put up his own hay.[65] (This would have been in the 1930s.)

Above: William Bird's barn held ninety tons of loose hay. William Bird is holding a team on the left; Lewis Bird is driving the wagon on the left; and Bob Bird is driving the team on the right, circa 1890. *Courtesy of Yampa-Egeria Museum.*

Left: Earle Moore riding a "teeter board" sweep rake, about 1920. *Herold family collection.*

Moore had this to say about the process, "The first two or three years, the haying was done using horsepower. We used two sweep rakes, one dump rake and the plunger team. Hawkins had a small tractor with which he did the mowing on his own place. We always prided ourselves, even though we were a small operation, we could stack as much loose hay in a day as anyone."

About the third year of stacking Hawkins's hay, Francis Moore converted a small Model A Ford truck into a power sweep rake. This replaced the two horse-powered sweeps. He then converted another Model A Ford truck into a dump rake by combining an old horse-drawn rake onto it. The first year, this particular machine was used as a mower, with the cutter bar mounted in front of the rear wheel. Later, the mowing machine was put on a small Ferguson tractor. The plunger was the only operation that still used horses. However, Moore still needed two good men on the haystack, and with World War II coming along, good men were scarce. Just about this same time, Hawkins sold the ranch to Wad Hinman, so there was no more hay contracting there.

Just after World War II, some land was traded, so the Henry Trantham meadow was now part of Francis Moore's operation. About this time, he started using a truck on the plunger. He bought a small tractor and mower, so everything in the hayfield was now motor-driven, no more horses. He also changed the rake to a double width by using hydraulics. This let him cover more ground with less people. In the mid-1960s, he started using a baler.

Francis Moore was enough of a mechanic and inventor to convert much of his own machinery. Other than that, the transition from horses to machinery was quite typical of the ranchers in the area and happened at about the same time.

Grain, mostly wheat, barley or oats, was another major crop grown by the first homesteaders. Grains provided fodder for animals as well as food for their families.

By the time the homesteaders came into South Routt, most people did not thresh grain by hand. Threshing machines were the preferred method of sorting grain from the straw. Very few people actually owned a threshing machine. (These were locally called separators.) When the grain was ready to harvest, each homesteader would cut the grain, form the cut stalks into bundles and then move the bundles to a stack. The grain could be left in this stack until the threshing machine could be moved to that location. The people who did own a machine would move them from one homestead to the next to separate the grain from the straw.

Right: Stacking hay with an "overshot" stacker, circa 1915. *Herold family collection.*

Middle: Keith Kirby at Red Dirt Divide riding a "dump" or "sulky" rake. *Courtesy of Hayne-Ray collection.*

Bottom: Steam engine and threshing machine with the crew to run them. *Herold family collection.*

Francis Moore was quite young when someone showed him how to tie a bundle of grain; perhaps it was Ed Outland, who was working for H.E. Moore at the time:

> *To use this type of tie for a bundle, two clumps of grain straws are used* [heads still attached]. *Each clump should be a "good handful" in size. One of these handfuls goes in each direction around the bundle of straw. A twist is made with the clump of grain to hold them together; this twist holds the bundle solid. Someone who has done this can make it look very easy to tie good solid bundles. Depending on the length of the straw, bundles could weigh anywhere from 60 pounds to more than 100 pounds.*[66]

During the First World War, H.E. Moore bought a steam tractor and separator; both were a Reeves make. The steam tractor was given the name "Old Maude."[67] H.E. spent a large amount of time threshing, in both the south end of the county as well as the Sidney and Twenty Mile areas. Many farmers planted wheat so they could "feed the army." One fall, it had gotten quite late, and there was a lot of ice and snow on the ground before H.E. brought his separator and tractor back to Yampa. He had worked his way, threshing as he went, as far as Middle Creek. Since the roads were so slick, he left the heavy steam tractor and thresher at Middle Creek rather than bring them over the steep hills to Yampa. The next spring, he went back and brought them home. The tractor traveled only "about as fast as a person could walk." (It covered about three or four miles per hour.)

It seems to have been fairly common for the early steam engines to have names. One engine was named "Old Sal." The name appeared in a document found in the agriculture files at the Tread of the Pioneers Museum in Steamboat Springs. The initials E.K. were the clues that identified the owner of the machine.

Elmer King bought a Case steam tractor in 1914. It had twenty-two-inch iron wheels and weighed thirteen tons when it was loaded with water and coal. He unloaded it off the train at Toponas. The tractor turned with a chain on the steering. According to the Tread of the Pioneers Museum Agriculture file, he "had to turn the wheel about 40 times to get it turned. Six miles per hour was as fast as we could go. The Coal bunkers carried about a ton of coal."

This fellow seems to have threshed in many different places around the valley. "I threshed above Steamboat and over Red Dirt Divide. Went pretty

Francis Moore, pictured here in 2004, standing in front of the type of steam engine that he used on his threshing machine in the 1920s. *Author's collection.*

near to Crosho Lake once." He could thresh 2,500 to 3,000 bushels a day and claimed to have threshed 10,000 bushels in three days.

Like many of the other operators around at the time, he had trouble moving the tractor and thresher from one place to another when the roads were icy and muddy. Old Sal's owner noted that one time during a storm he left the machine sit beside the road for three weeks. Another time, the tractor slipped off one side of the road and the thresher went off the other side. He noted that after the road dried, it wasn't too difficult to pull it out.

Francis Moore graduated from high school in 1928, and the next year, he bought a threshing machine and started threshing grain for different people around the area. Don Manning was his "separator man."[68] Manning was good with machines and had "a great deal of experience" with threshing machines.

The Alfred boys had raised a crop of oats on their place up the river (southwest of Yampa on County Road 7). Francis Moore threshed the grain for them in 1930. Don Manning shoveled the weed seed out of the way so the rest of the weeds had a place to fall. Moore recalled, "We had a pile of weed seed about eighteen inches high."

Mrs. Alfred came out and looked into the bin—it was straight oats. She commented, "Oh, what a beautiful crop of oats, there was no weeds in it this year." Don Manning just looked at Moore but did not show her the pile of weed seed on the ground. When another Yampa operator threshed for the Alfreds, he would put a board over the screen in the thresher. This let the weed seed go into the bin with the oats. People paid threshing costs on the grain that was in their bins, not on the time it took to thresh. If weed seeds were left in with the grain, it made more to measure.

That same year, 1930, Moore was operating his thresher up by Toponas. He went to Kaiser's to thresh. Kaiser told Moore that they could measure the bin before they started to thresh and then measure it after they put the grain into it so they "would both know how much grain the bin held." Moore responded that they did not really need to do that. No one had ever complained of having a "full measure" when he was doing the work. Kaiser did not pursue it, and after the threshing was done, he was fully satisfied with the measure. Moore found out that Kaiser had had a fight the year before over settlement of the amount of grain when someone else had done his threshing.

Each grain owner fed the threshing crews their noon meal. When a threshing machine came to a farm, the neighbors would come to help. Commonly, the crews were a mix of neighbors and the men who traveled with the machine. Often the neighboring wives would also come to help fix and serve the meals.

Arden and Ada Huffstetler were two people that Francis Moore liked to work for when he was running the separator.[69] He said that Ada was a great cook and always expected the threshing crew to enjoy their meals. Arden and Ada had two boys, Buford and Ben.

One year, Moore had his threshing machine at Huffstetler's during the last of November. The weather was good, so the fellows decided to thresh even though it was Thanksgiving Day. Ada, along with the other women who were helping her, cooked turkey, dressing and an entire holiday meal for all the men in the threshing crew. Moore recalled they certainly enjoyed eating that meal.

Another time when Moore was threshing on the mesa west of Finger Rock, he lost his billfold. This was during the Great Depression, when no one had very much money. The next morning, before Moore realized he had lost his billfold, Buford Huffstetler and his brother, Ben, returned that wallet. At the time, the boys were young, probably somewhere in their early teens. Moore said that when he opened the billfold, there was nothing missing—he didn't think anyone had even opened it. It had a couple dollars in it, so he gave the cash to the boys for finding and returning the billfold.

Each year before Moore started to take his separator around to the different farms, he bought four new pairs of pliers.[70] He could always plan to lose about that many pairs. Each pair cost nine cents. They were not smoothed up, just rough from the cast, but worked as well as the ones that had been smoothed.

One fall (probably in 1925) a crew was threshing grain at a homestead in Terhune Basin.[71] The owner's name was John. (Francis Moore couldn't remember the last name.) John ran out of sacks to put his grain into, but another fellow said that he had some extras. They sent Melvin Burris, a sixteen-year-old kid, down to get them. They had all been told not to drive on the road through John Kennedy's place anymore, so when his father pointed down the road that direction, Melvin asked if he was to go that way or the much longer road around.

John said, "Oh, just explain to him what you are after and that we need them in a hurry, and I don't think you'll have any trouble." Melvin did not have any trouble getting the sacks, but evidently, John Kennedy saw him go through and was waiting for him on the way back. Melvin had just opened a gate and carried it back so he could drive through. To get the gate out of the way, he had jumped up on a small bank about eighteen inches to two feet high. Just then, Kennedy came up to him and started yelling and "roaring like a bear." Melvin said he could not understand a word he was saying. Melvin tried to explain, but Kennedy just kept coming toward him and continued to "roar." Melvin had the advantage of being on that embankment, so when Kennedy got close, Melvin hit him. Kennedy fell down into the road but got up and came at Melvin again, still roaring and yelling. Melvin hit him in the face once more. This happened several times until finally Kennedy got tired and went away.

The next day, someone saw Kennedy at the depot when he took his cream can in to send out to the creamery. John had two black eyes, and his whole face was swollen and bruised. When asked, "My gosh man, what happened to you?" John just grunted and would not say a word about what had happened. Later, the same fellow saw Melvin, who did not have a mark on him. Everyone thought this was a good story, because Melvin was just a teenage kid.

There were other threshing machines in the south end of the county during the 1920s and 1930s. One was run by Wade Davis; another was pulled by Jim Whaley. Undoubtedly, there were others as well. Francis Moore told the following story:

> *One time I was pulling our thresher toward home with the twenty Cat out on the Crosho Lake road. Jim Whaley had evidently just finished threshing on a place with his machine and pulled out behind me, also heading back toward Yampa. I was ahead of Jim and had gained some when I got to the long hill there at the Joe Rossi place. I kept gaining until Jim started down the hill. He threw his tractor out of gear to catch up. His machine was bouncing and jumping all over the road, I thought it was going to bounce right off the road. It did stay on the road and he made it to the bottom of that hill right behind me.*

The newspaper had the following stories about some of the different grain fields in 1905. If someone raised a good crop of grain, they would bring a sample into town to show it off and to brag to all their neighbors. They were genuinely proud of what their hard work had accomplished.

"Some brome grass measuring 5 feet tall was brought in recently by S. K. Price and placed on exhibition at the Bank of Yampa. The seed was sown last year and was grown on the Nelson Nesbitt ranch above town by Mr. Price. The yield of seed would be enormous and the stalks are none too large to make good feed."[72]

"J.T. Roup this week brought in a sample of barley which was raised on his ranch in Smith Basin, about 8 miles above town. It measures 3 feet 4 inches in height, is well headed and well filled, and was raised without irrigation. Just step into the Bank of Yampa and take a look at it."[73]

"Jack Roup was in Tuesday from his ranch on Five Pine Mesa. He reports a splendid crop of oats, grown without irrigation. Some of them are 6 feet tall."[74]

LETTUCE BECAME AN EXTREMELY important crop to Egeria Park starting in 1921 and continued in a limited manner through the 1950s.

In 1924, there were only a few packing sheds by the railroad tracks near Yampa. By 1927, the sheds were located at intervals along the railroad tracks from Yampa to Finger Rock. Above Finger Rock at Trappers Siding, there were two packing sheds, as well as ice sheds and an ice pond. The ice from the pond was cut in the winter and then placed into the large icehouses. The next summer, during the lettuce harvest, the ice was put into the railroad cars to preserve the produce. There were more packing sheds at Toponas.

"[The year] 1921 seems to be the beginning of the lettuce in this area. Frank and John Kenley and Fred Halstead used a small tract of land on the Wheeler brother's ranch; they shipped three cars of lettuce and got $3,000."[75]

According to informational development sheets, there were 113 railroad cars of lettuce sent out in 1922. In 1923, Yampa sent out 192 carloads, Trappers Siding sent 26 cars and Toponas had 16 carloads. The lettuce was still going strong in 1927.

In 1922, the newspaper reported that to produce the best-quality lettuce, it should be raised at an altitude of about eight thousand feet.[76] This was what made the conditions of the lettuce fields in Routt County so favorable.

When thinking of Yampa's and South Routt's experience with raising head lettuce, Francis Moore did not think "the big boom" lasted more than ten or fifteen years.[77]

"Finley Strine started the whole explosion, he rented one acre from Johnny Hughes and planted it to Head Lettuce." (This would have been in 1920.) He cared for it very carefully and cut four hundred crates of

Lettuce crates stacked on a wagon to be taken to the railroad. *Courtesy of Yampa-Egeria Museum, Fogg Collection.*

Workers ready to hoe the weeds in a field west of Eagle Rock. *Courtesy of Yampa-Egeria Museum, Macfarlane Collection.*

lettuce, which he shipped by rail express and cleared $3 per crate—$1,200 from one acre. Immediately, everyone wanted to get into the raising of head lettuce. At the peak, there were six separate packing companies shipping head lettuce out of Yampa, another at Trappers Siding and two at Toponas.

Francis Moore told this story about his first experience working in the lettuce industry at age thirteen:

> *My first job with the lettuce was a "crate knocker" as they were known. [The summer of 1923] I nailed the "shook" (bundled pieces of wood cut to size for the crates) into finished crates. Each evening after school and on Saturdays and Sundays, Carey Trantham, Arthur Russell and I hammered crates together for John Cole. I nailed the ends while the two other boys nailed the sides and bottom. I got one cent for each end; Carey and Arthur got three cents for their part; five cents for the finished crate. On a good day, we could "knock together" 200 crates—$10.00 was big money! As a man's wages at the time was a dollar a day.*

Al Dilly came from Arizona and was a "professional" crate knocker.[78] He was the "fastest crate knocker" anyone in the area had seen. He married a local, Margaret Hughes, when she graduated from high school. They followed the lettuce industry back toward the Arizona fields.

A lettuce field just north of Yampa. Henry Page is on the right. *Courtesy of Yampa-Egeria Museum.*

Lola Smith (her father was Hugh) also married a crate knocker from Arizona. Some of the older women tried to warn her not to marry. She answered them by saying, "I know my onions!"

During the early days of the head lettuce craze, Irvin Shorter built a crate mill right beside H.E. Moore's sawmill, about a mile up Lawson Creek on Greenridge.[79] H.E. sawed the logs into four-inch cants (square rough-cut pieces) then shot them across to Irv's crate mill on rollers. The cants were first sawn to crate length then run through gang saws to make the slats and end pieces for the crates. Those pieces were then packed into bundles of fifty or more, called shook. That worked well for three or four years; then the lettuce companies changed from the LA crate, which Irv Shorter had been making, to the Brawley crate. For Shorter to change would have taken different machinery. In addition, he could not compete with the prices the lettuce companies would allow. The companies were shipping carload lots of crates into Yampa from big outside mills. The lettuce craze had begun to slow down in Yampa anyway, so Shorter took his family and moved back to Michigan.

After the initial lettuce sales, the packing companies started putting ice into the railroad cars to help keep the lettuce fresh. J.R. Espy of the Espy Ice Company visited the Yampa Valley to choose a site for building icehouses.[80] The site chosen was at Trapper's Siding, just south of Finger

Rock, where a large pond was created with a four-foot dike.[81] Water was diverted into the pond from Beaver Creek. This pond would then freeze during the winter, and the ice was cut and stored in sheds. The ice was cut into two-by-four-foot blocks, eighteen to twenty-four inches thick. This ice would remain frozen until summer, when it was shaved and blown into railroad cars of lettuce and spinach. This ice industry lasted until the 1950s, when it was believed that the ice from open ponds was not clean enough to be placed on food items.[82]

Francis Moore said a group from India came into Routt County when much of the land was being put into head lettuce (in 1927 or 1928).[83] Many of them had the last name Sing. The only names that Moore could remember were Susha Sing, Takkar Sing and Sindar Sing. After he graduated from high school, Moore worked for Susha Sing. Moore bought a small crawler tractor, and he was plowing the ground for Susha. Francis asked Susha if all the men were related, since they were all named Sing. Susha told him that they were named for the area from which they came. Francis would be "Francis Routt County."

Each of the Indians that came into the area had five rented acres of land that was "in his own name." However, they all helped one another clear the ground and take care of the crop. One of the Sings (he was a young fellow) was very slender, but he was extremely strong. When they were clearing the

Ice sheds at Trapper's Siding in 1980. *Courtesy of Wanda (Gumpreht) Redmond.*

ground of rocks, he would "sit on his heels"; the rest of the people would roll a large rock onto his lap. He would then stand up and carry that rock to the side of the field.

Takkar Sing was the "boss" for them all. He was "quite smart" and had John Cole make contracts for each of them working the ground. They were tight contracts that stated when all the deadline dates were, how fine the ground was to be plowed and so on:

> *The first year I was out of school, I worked for a Hindu, Susha Sing. With a tractor and machinery, I was to prepare five acres of raw sagebrush land "ready for seeding." This was on the mesa of Pollard Carnahan's place and it was to be completed by June 15. It sounded easy, but rainy weather and a few other things held me up. Before the deadline date, I was starting at daybreak and working until full dark—about 16 hours. That was the longest days I can remember putting in on a tractor seat....*
>
> *The Hindus stopped for a service or prayer occasionally, it was not every day; I am not sure whether it was a certain day of the week or just on special occasions. The field where I was working must have been the furthest away; when a truck would come to the edge of the field, there were already several people (at least 10 or 15) in the back of the truck and they would jump out as the truck stopped. The ones working in the field would stop whatever they were doing, and run towards the truck. When everyone got there, they would hold a meeting for twenty or thirty minutes, then everyone would go back to work at whatever they had been doing.*[84]

When Francis Moore was preparing the land to plant, he used an A frame made out of railroad rails to cut off the sagebrush before he started to plow. Tony Loranti had worked as a section boss for the railroad, so he knew where to find used pieces of rail to make the A frame. It was already at Pollard Carnahan's place, so Moore was able to use it without any loss of time. The main leg of the frame was about ten feet long and pulled almost straight behind the tractor. The other leg of the frame sat at about a thirty-degree angle. On the bottom of this leg, Loranti had welded plow shears to help cut off the sagebrush. Moore said that this apparatus worked quite well.

Many people benefited from the lettuce boom. Mike Yurich, historian at Oak Creek, told of residents that traveled to the lettuce sheds to work at packing. Mike's mother, Rose, was one of the ones who worked in the packing sheds. Each morning during the lettuce packing season, Rose Yurich, Agnes Harvey and many other women and girls rode the train from Oak Creek to

Yampa to work in the packing sheds.[85] They were able to make higher wages packing than performing other jobs that were available to them.

Fred Mohr commented that he raised his lettuce and spinach at nine thousand feet elevation and depended entirely on rain for moisture.[86] When he thinned lettuce, he used a short-handled hoe, which made for backbreaking work. At one time, he had twenty women and children helping in his fields. In his own spare time, he and Rayburn Gibson hired out to help other ranchers thin their lettuce.

Margaret Rossi said that lettuce helped her family pay off their ranch better than cattle or hay ever did.[87] The problem with raising lettuce was that it was difficult to cultivate; it required "stoop labor." They had to bend over to plant, thin, weed or harvest the crops. They would field pack the lettuce to take it into the packing sheds in Yampa where it was repacked and put on ice.

Agnes Harvey, age fourteen, standing in front of lettuce crates, September 7, 1926. *Courtesy of Tracks & Trails Museum.*

When H.E. Moore was growing lettuce during the 1920s, he felt that the long-handled hoe was just as efficient a tool as the short-handled hoe and certainly easier on the back.[88] Some of the lettuce growers felt the short-handled hoe (the handle was about eighteen inches long) was better for thinning the lettuce and weeding close to the young plants.

Wanda (Gumphrect) Redmond explained during her talk at the Brown Bag Luncheon for the Tread of the Pioneers Museum that she liked a long-handled hoe for weeding lettuce and spinach. As a teenager, she worked in her father's fields near Toponas.

Some have said that the disease "slime" was the cause for ending lettuce growing in this area.[89] It is true some of the old fields—those where lettuce had been returned year after year—were getting a slime mold, but new fields were still raising good lettuce. Herb Moore plowed up an old alfalfa field, planted five acres and raised the best, soundest heads of lettuce they had ever grown; every head was perfect. But the market was completely gone.

The Gerard Company came and looked at that wonderful field and said it would take a chance and give Herb one dollar per pack-out crate. If the company cleared more, it would give him more. However, Gerard said it did not even get enough to pay the freight. So, that was the end of head lettuce for the Gerard Company and also for Herb and Francis Moore.

After the market for lettuce failed in the 1930s, a few landowners continued growing lettuce or else converted their ground to growing spinach. The Crowner family of Yampa and the Otto Gumphrect family in Toponas were able to raise both lettuce and spinach until the early 1950s.[90] Near Toponas, Jack Holden was one of the larger spinach growers to stay in production into the 1950s. In 1946, Jack Holden was called "Colorado's Spinach King."[91] The newspaper article stated that Holden owned twelve farms and employed four hundred people during the harvest season.

Above: Lettuce or spinach crates loaded on trucks at Toponas, circa 1935. *Courtesy of the Crowner family.*

Opposite, top: "Four abreast team" pulling a potato digger. *Courtesy of Yampa-Egeria Museum, Fogg Collection.*

Opposite, bottom: These fellows are picking up, sorting and sacking potatoes. *Courtesy of Yampa-Egeria Museum, Fogg Collection.*

Potatoes were one of the most important crops the first homesteaders planted when they came into the valley. Many of those early families were quite large, with eight or more children. Potatoes and other root vegetables could be stored for use during the long winters when other food could not be obtained.

> *Cap. Lampshire has the finest potatoes in Yampa, and he says he didn't plant them in the moon, either....The Cap. has some theories of his own regarding the science of gardening. In the first place, he is very careful about selecting his potatoes for seed. He is especially particular to see that the ones with good eyes are selected. Those with cross-eyes, sore eyes or moon-eyes,*

YAMPA VALLEY'S LOST EGERIA PARK

he discards. He has an oculist paid by the year to examine and treat the eyes of his potatoes, and in that way keeps them in excellent condition. In several cases it has been found necessary to order spectacles for his potatoes to correct some defect in vision. By looking carefully after the optics of his potatoes, he has enabled them to see when spring is really here and they may, with safety to themselves, come up.[92]

Other articles proclaimed, "A few tons of potatoes for sale, 1 cent per pound.[93] Another offered, "25 stacks of hay. Inquire of Peter Simon."

"Grandpa Bird brought some potatoes to the *Yampa Leader* office; one weighed two pounds five ounces. Another weighed three pounds ten ounces. The larger one was eight and one-half inches long and twenty-one inches around the largest way."[94] The article also stated that they were solid and certainly beauties. They were raised without irrigation at the north end of Yampa.

When those first settlers came into the valley, most of them had the idea that potatoes would not grow in the bottom of the valley; potatoes could only be planted in the good rich "quaker" [quaking aspen] soil. Robert Laughlin was a firm believer of planting potatoes on both sides of the valley, if they froze in one place; perhaps they would grow in another. He had ten growing children to feed during those long winters.

One year when his sons, Tom and Bob, were young teenagers, perhaps in 1896 or 1897, Robert decided to plant another patch of potatoes "up in the quakers on Greenridge." He still had several sacks of seed potatoes left that could be planted. He loaded the seed and his sons, into the back of a wagon early one morning. It was spring, the snow was melting and the Yampa River was in flood stage. The boys were tired of planting potatoes and knew that if all that they had planted grew there was going to be a lot of work in the fall to dig those potatoes. They were sure that their father was planting too many! Since the river was so high, Robert had his full attention on the team of horses and getting them to cross the river at the ford.

While Robert was occupied, the boys dumped a couple sacks of potatoes into the river so they would have less to plant. I never did hear what Robert said when they reached the "potato patch" and were short a couple sacks to be planted.

Jack Terhune lived east of Finger Rock in what was called Terhune Basin. He raised different types of crops and vegetables, but one of his main ways

A large garden was necessary for the early families. From left to right are Mary, William, Bob, Lewis, Jessie and Della Bird. *Herold family collection.*

of making money was selling seed potatoes.[95] Seed potatoes are potatoes to be cut into pieces and planted to grow a new crop. He was able to sell these for a little more money than he would have gotten for just "eating" potatoes. He sold these seed potatoes to people in other areas as well as locally. (About 1990, Carl Herold met an older fellow who lived near Greeley, Colorado. When this fellow was ten years old, he had come to the Terhune ranch with his father to buy seed potatoes.)

To keep these potatoes in good shape, Terhune built a large cellar. It was built into the hillside in the typical fashion.[96] The difference with Terhune's cellar was the front wall. It was made of octagonal rocks that he had picked up and stacked into place.

Louie Rossi raised potatoes near Oak Creek; he had a wide market and was able to keep and store the potatoes in a large cellar for sale in the winter. There was even a variety of potato called the "Rossi" potato. The cellar was located where the present high school football field is now.

Two or three years after the first homesteaders arrived, the families learned to plant large gardens and also use many of the indigenous foods around them. One of those was the yampa root, which had been a favorite of the Utes.

Another was the dandelion plant. When the dandelion leaves first came up in the spring, many homesteaders used them for salads. Evelyn Pidcock commented, "After a long winter, that first taste of green was always good. We also ate the dandelion blooms. I like them the best when they are battered and fried."[97]

Pigweed and lambsquarters were also utilized. These were treated as greens and used much like spinach.

The native berries were prized for making jellies, jams and even pies. They included gooseberries, wild currants, thimbleberries, wild raspberries, wild strawberries, chokecherries and sarvis berries. (This was the local spelling for the berry and gave Sarvis Creek its name.)

There was a forest fire a few years before the Laughlin family came into the valley. Both wild raspberries and wild strawberries were abundant in that burned-over area. Several of the families would go camping for a week at "their berry patch." They picked berries and boiled them at their campsite. This gave them preserves for their wintertime biscuits.

There were many different garden crops that the homesteaders planted and enjoyed. The following stories include some of the different crops but certainly not all.

The Laughlin family "coming home from the strawberry patch" about 1897. *Herold family collection.*

One spring, Jack Terhune was plowing his garden plot to get it ready for replanting.[98] He turned the rows of last year's parsnips over. (As was normal, they had been left in the ground over the winter so the freezing would sweeten them.) He had more parsnips than his family could eat, so he took the extras to the M&A Market in Yampa to trade with Howard Allen. Allen was happy to buy them.

> *"Good looking parsnips, Jack, I'll pay you seven cents a pound for them," offered Howard. Jack said that sounded good, so he sold them to Howard.*
> *Jack was still standing at the counter when a fellow came into the store and exclaimed, "Parsnips—How much do you want for them?"*
> *"Fifteen cents a pound," replied Howard without any hesitation.*
> *Jack said he could understand Howard doubling the price, but he wanted to know what the extra penny was for!*

The King family (no relation to the Preston King family in Toponas) lived on what is now Routt County Road 21 southeast of the cemetery.[99] Robert Laughlin had sold about ten acres for a house site. King started a strawberry patch in the small valley west of the cemetery, and he did quite well with them. They were good strawberries, and he was able to trade or sell them to the grocery store in Yampa. They had a son, Ralph, who attended the school in Yampa with Francis Moore in the second and third grades.

The King family traded with Charlie and Nan Sanders: the King place in Routt County for the Sanders place in Arkansas. Charlie Sanders had no interest in the strawberries; he did not irrigate or weed them, so they quickly stopped producing.

Fred Mohr had this to say about the raising of strawberries: "One year [during the 1930s], I planted one-quarter acre of strawberries. They produced very well. We sold all we could pick to the grocery stores for 25 cents a quart, which we thought was a good price."[100]

Even the people who lived within the town of Yampa planted gardens. The following excerpts came from the Ruth Cole journal.

> *June 1, 1948, Went to Oak Creek after cabbage plants. Cold and some snow.*
> *June 3, 1948, Set out cabbage plants.*
> *July 2, 1949, Worked in garden all morning. Baked cake in afternoon.*
> *Mark and Dad went fishing. Tom and Dad here for supper.*
> *October 1, 1949, Cut cabbage and made krout [sic]. Tom and Mark helped in evening.*

June 4, 1950, Got the ground ready and made garden.
June 5, 1950, Made garden in the morning. Went fishing in afternoon. Good Luck.
September, 7, 1950, I ironed all morning. Canned beets in the afternoon.
September 17, 1950, Made choke cherry jell. Pearl brought me some [chokecherries] from Callies.
September 23, 1951, Weather not so nice. Mark dug potatoes in morning.
May 26, 1952, Made garden all day long. Tired and went to bed early.
May 27, 1952, Ironed all morning—Mark and Dad Cole planted potatoes.
September 2, 1952, Made cucumber and beet pickles. Weather real nice.
September 4, 1952, Made bread and butter pickles in the morning."
September 5, 1952, Made beet pickles[101]

In years when the summer rains came just at the right time, the homesteaders were able to grow dry land crops on ground that had no irrigation. However, Francis Moore said that only one year out of five was all that a person could depend on getting a good crop. The other four would either be too dry or else a freeze would stunt the crop. Because of this, water and water rights became very important to all the homesteaders in the area.

Mark and Ruth Cole, circa 1950. *Herold family collection.*

A noteworthy incident happened with one of the fellows who farmed near the Burnt Mesa ditch.[102] Even then, water seemed to be worth a fight:

A man named Huffman was renting the Fisher place. He had planted a small field with oats. The Burnt Mesa ditch looped through the property just above his field. A ground squirrel dug a hole in the lower ditch bank causing a leak, which soon enlarged until it was draining half the water in the ditch. This washed out a streak of grain completely across the small field.

Huffman, apparently short tempered anyway, was going to collect damages even sue all the ditch owners. At that time, the owners were Tom Woods, Grant Hemerley, Cecil Long and Francis Moore. They all gathered there, not only to see the damage, but also to repair the ditch. Huffman was very mad. As the ditch owners observed the damage, Tom Woods told Huffman to calm down; they would pay him for the damage done.

But, Grant Hemerley said, "I am not in favor of paying, who knows, Huffman may make another hole in the bank just to collect damages." Huffman jerked out a knife and began advancing toward Grant.

Grant slapped his hand on his hip pocket and said, "You take one more step and I will blow your head off." The threat worked! Huffman stopped.

Then Tom Woods calmly said, "Now, let's all put our play things away and let's talk this thing out." He then looked at Huffman and asked, "Just how many bushels do you think were washed out?"

Huffman looked at the narrow streak washed across the field, tried to figure how many bundles of grain would have been there, then how many bundles to make a bushel, and finally came up with one bushel.

At that point, Tom asked, "You mean we were going to kill each other over one bushel of grain?" When putting it that way, it did seem ridiculous even to Huffman, who said as long as it did not happen again, he would forget it.

On the way home Cecil said to Grant, "I was afraid you were going to pull that tobacco can clear out of your pocket back there."

Grant replied, "My knees were shaking, there is nothing that scares me like a knife, I think I could face a gun better than a knife."

Cecil and Francis were talking later; neither of them thought Grant even owned a gun, but his bluff had worked with Huffman.

In his manuscript about the Crossan family, George Charles Crossan had this to say about the importance of water rights. On November 9, 1904, the Macfarlane and Crossan ditch was approved.[103] The original ditch was used to water the Macfarlanes' and Crossans' meadows. George Crossan had the first and third water rights out of the ditch. "This project was what made the Crossan' ranch one of the most productive cattle ranches in Egeria Park."

Water for all the different crops has always been important to the farmers and ranchers of the western United States. It was certainly no different for any of the crops grown in the Egeria Park area. Some of the small grain fields were cultivated without the benefit of irrigation, but most of the hay fields and many of the lettuce fields depended on having supplemental water. Even the gardens had to have irrigation to be sure to grow enough food for the winter months.

5

SAWMILLS AND LUMBERJACKS

The timber industry has been a big part of Egeria Park from the time the first homesteaders came into the valley in the 1880s. Those first families used logs for their homes. Many came from the Missouri area and were adept with tools used in working timber (broadaxes, crosscut saws, cant hooks and so on) The availability of good lumber in the region influenced the Yampa area from the 1880s until mid-1900. The early lumberjacks and sawyers used manpower, horsepower and some waterpower for their energy. By the 1930s and 1940s, the industry had changed to the use of steam power and gasoline trucks. This development ended the small one- or two-person mills and created the larger mills along the railroad and main highways. However, since the trees in this altitude do not grow as quickly or as large as timber in other regions, the sawmills were never big corporate industries. A few of the people making lumber production possible in Upper and Lower Egeria are included in the following accounts.

Hiram Gardner ran the first sawmill in the Egeria area in 1886. His mill was located up "the Bear River" toward the Flattops and used water as the power source to turn the saws.[104] This man gave his name to Gardner Park and Gardner Reservoir.

The Bird sawmill started in 1888. This first Bird Mill was also located up the Bear River. (The headwaters of the Yampa River were settled in the early 1880s, so the timber near the Flattops was close to the settlers.)

In 1902, the shingle mill operated by John Phillips was up and running. It was located on the Phillips homestead just west of Finger Rock. Shingles from this mill were used for the original roof of the Congregational church built in 1902 on Moffat Avenue in Yampa.[105] Phillips's mill was run with waterpower; Phillips ran a ditch to the edge of the low mesa behind his house.

In 1905, the Roland and Lazarus Sawmill moved its boiler and the last of its machinery to a point about halfway between Pyramid and Yampa. "The new location is within the White River Reserve, the owners have arrangements to purchase mature trees; no trees less than 18 inches are to be taken."[106]

At the area on Greenridge called the Swede Camp where the U.S. Forest Service Road 285 crosses Mill Creek, the fellows who did the lumbering at the site did all their work with broadaxes.[107] They were cutting ties for the railroad, probably during the winter of 1907 and spring of 1908. Much of the work was done during the winter, so they used sled bunks and hauled the ties down to the railroad right of way. Since the ties were cut with the axes, there was no mill used. The Swedes cut the ties to size and shaped them right where they felled the trees; this left broadaxe shavings lying all through the trees. These shavings were good tinder for a forest fire that ran through the area a few years later.

There were several logging and sawmill camps on the Hunt Creek drainages west of Yampa. These began in the latter 1880s, and a few remained as late as the 1950s. The lumber from these was used locally until the railroad came. The railroad gave the timber industry in the entire valley a new market.

William Bird and some of his sons operated a sawmill in at least two locations under the Little Flattops on the South Hunt Creek drainage. Albert Bird and his brother, Frank Bird, brought timber into Egeria Park from those locations. Some of the lumber was for their own use; some was sold to their neighbors.

Some of the lumber camps that Floyd "Dutch" Viele heard about or remembered include the following:[108]

- The Berg Mill was at the head of Middle Hunt Creek and was operated by George Berg, then by the Bartholomews.
- The Mill Creek Mill was on the west side of Bellyache Mountain.
- The Bird Mill was on South Hunt Creek; it was operated at the turn of the century.
- The Bell Mill was located on North Hunt Creek and was owned by Ed Bell and his brother Sam. Ed ran the mill until his death; his son took over until he died four months later. (These are

the same Bell brothers who built the Bell and Canant Store in Yampa and had the Bell Lumber Yard and Bell Mercantile in Oak Creek.) Dutch's father, Jeff Viele, operated the Bell Mill from 1928 through 1934.

- The Holts had a steam-powered mill on Little Oak Creek in the 1940s and 1950s.
- A man named Citron had a portable diesel-powered mill on Little Oak Creek.
- Another portable mill was located near the present Allen Basin Reservoir. (Dutch did not name the owner of this mill.)
- Earl Jones had a mill on lower Hunt Creek about a quarter of a mile south of the town of Phippsburg.

Dutch said that his father quit the logging and sawmill business in 1934 for several reasons.[109] One reason was the Great Depression. Then, there were fewer marketable logs, and it was getting harder to keep up with the forest service regulations. When the rule came out that the mill folks could no longer graze their horses and milk cows on the forest land, Jeff thought it was time to do other things. He leased land so he could ranch and farm.

Later, Dutch and some of his brothers operated a sawmill at their Hunt Creek ranch, where they sawed house logs. "This mill was powered by the PTO belt from the 'ole Massey,'" said Dutch, with a proud smile.[110]

Herb Moore said that in the early 1900s, the Sarvis Creek Lumber Company was one of those things that looked good on paper but did not work in practice.[111] The idea was to use water to move the logs to the mill. (The mill was located on a small island in the town of Steamboat Springs. Later, Dillan Rich built a flour mill near the same location.) Lumber companies did it in other places where there was more water and the hills were not as steep. The company expected to float logs from upper Sarvis Creek to its mill in Steamboat Springs. It built a flume by the side of Sarvis Creek that was to carry one log at a time and shoot it down to the Yampa River. The flume was extremely steep, and the logs traveled so fast that some jumped completely out of the chute, while others would break the sides of the flume. When the flume did get some of the logs to the Yampa River, the logs were prone to start pileups at bends in the river, causing a jam. This would raise the water so the logs would then go over the riverbank and end up in someone's meadow. In other words, everything went wrong that could.

A mill on the north end of Greenridge, located about a mile north of Whipple Park, was run by the American Timber Company. This sawmill took lumber off the north end of the ridge. A few years after this mill finished work in the area, a forest fire went through. This burned-out area then became known locally as the "American Timber Claim Burn."

At one time, Herb Moore and two brothers from Nebraska, possibly named Fram, formed the White Pine Lumber Company.[112] For a short time, they ran three sawmills on Greenridge. It must have been about 1918 or 1919. The first mill was on Lawson Creek about one and a half miles up the creek from Highway 131. It was where the small stream comes into Lawson Creek from the south. Mill number 2 was up Lawson Creek about two more miles where a small stream joins Lawson Creek from the north. Mill number 3 was about a half mile above the Pink Easterly homestead, just short of the U.S. Forest Service boundary. The company got into financial trouble, with the creditors demanding immediate payment. (Correlating this to other events, it would have been in 1920.) The two brothers saw their chance to cut their losses and duck out, so the company went into bankruptcy. This forced Moore into bankruptcy also. Eventually, his creditors were all paid at least a portion of what was owed them.

After a few years, Moore managed to get another sawmill started in the same location as the third mill site. He ran that mill for several years—until the usable timber was gone in the area.

Herb Moore also ran a mill at the upper end of Lawson Creek just east of Bison Park.[113] This area burned about 1948. Francis Moore used his Caterpillar tractor to help create a firebreak. At the time, this fire was the hottest ever recorded by the U.S. Forest Service. It killed much of the seed that was on and in the ground, so the trees did not come back as soon as they normally would. Some of the area was reseeded naturally; some of the area was replanted later by the forest service.

Many years ago, when horses were used exclusively for everything, including timber, Herb Moore did most of his timber work in the winter, because snow helped a great deal, especially in moving logs to the sawmill.[114] The sawmill was always in a lower area than the timber, thus all logs moved downhill. By using just the front runners and bunk of a sled, logs were loaded with about one-third of the log on the sled and two-thirds left to drag behind. This made a wide, packed, solid snow road. A single team, when shod with sharp shoes, could move a lot of logs—more lumber than they could haul using a high-wheel wagon with steel rims on dry ground.

Top: One of H.E. Moore's sawmills on Greenridge, 1926. *Herold family collection.*

Bottom: Logs ready to be rolled down to the sawmill, circa 1920. *Courtesy of Yampa-Egeria Museum, Fogg Collection.*

One year, Herb had a contract to supply the railroad with several thousand ties, in two sizes, 9″x9″x8½′ for use on the main lines and 7″x8″x8′ used on side tracks. The ties were to be stacked in square piles at Shorter's Spur for inspection by the railroad company. The railroad then shipped them to Denver for creosote. Shorter's Spur was the little side track just east of the

Laughlin buildings. The ties were stacked on the corner between County Road 21A and the railroad. After Francis Moore finished high school, he spent several winters hauling ties from the sawmill and stacking them on that corner ready for inspection. They had to be stacked exactly according to instructions, loosely, so the inspector could see all sides of each tie. When the Moores got about two thousand ties in piles, they would call for inspection. There were several pages of instruction on how they must be piled; also, there could be no bark or knots where spikes were to be driven as the rails crossed the tie. If the inspector saw a defect in a tie, he took a hammer and struck the end, leaving a red R (meaning reject) deeply indented in the wood. One nice sunny day, Moore and the inspector were just visiting after an inspection when the inspector made the statement, "If we inspectors don't cull a certain percent of the ties we inspect, the company doesn't think we are doing our job." After that, it didn't hurt Francis's conscience to look the ties over carefully—if he could find no defect, he would take his saw and cut off about a half inch of the end where the little red R was stamped and add it to his pile for the next inspection.

John Geer was good at running a saw; he worked for H.E. Moore at times but also ran mills of his own. John had a mill on the road east of the Pink Easterly homestead; it was about three-quarters of a mile west of the Bison Park reservoir. He also ran at least one mill near the Little Flattops. Kate Anderson worked as a cook for the mill on Greenridge before she married John Geer.

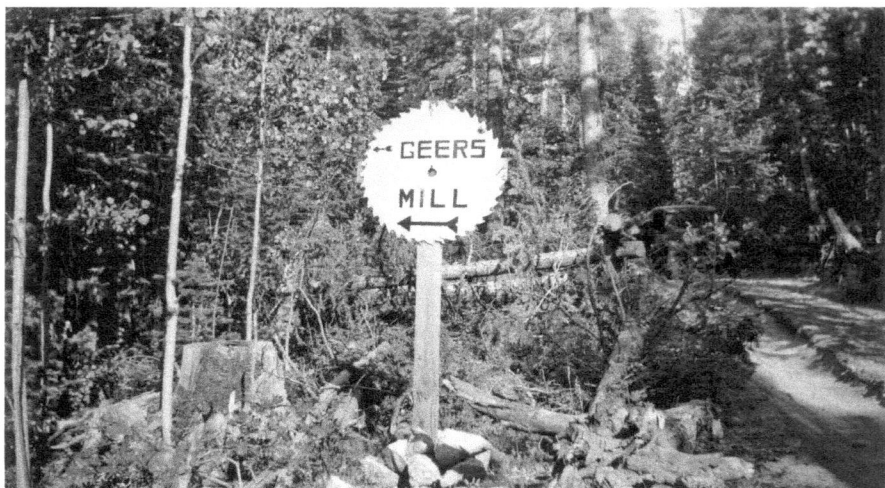

Sign in the forest painted on a used sawblade. *Courtesy of Yampa-Egeria Museum, Fogg Collection.*

John Geer, L.L. Wilson and his wife, Dora, enjoy the Pioneer Picnic in Yampa, 1937. *Courtesy of Yampa-Egeria Museum.*

One of the biggest dangers any mill faced was fire. A mill could catch fire from sparks in or around the saw; it could catch from sparks from the smokestack of the steam boiler or even from spontaneous combustion in the sawdust pile near the buildings. Sometimes this would smolder for several days before it was noticed. There was also the danger of someone throwing out a careless match or cigarette. Many of the mills in the area had fires at least once.

Francis Moore told this story about John Seivers, a prominent businessman in Yampa:

> *John Seivers had some timber about a half-mile south of Bison Park, on a little bench where it breaks off into Wheeler Basin. It was smaller timber so he got a contract to put it into ties. There was no road to it, so he made a deal with Bill Brown, an Arkansawyer, who had two grown boys and a portable mill. Brown was to get a set amount for each tie cut and stacked for drying. John thought he was being really shrewd, no mention of a road; but he figured that Brown would have to make one in order to get his mill and provisions in. Brown's mill was built on steel skids, so he just slid it down that steep bank to the little flat where the timber was, cut four stumps just*

One of John Geer's mills burned in 1937. *Courtesy of Yampa-Egeria Museum, Fogg Collection.*

the right height, set the mill on them and went to work. When he and the boys had cut all the trees big enough for ties, and had the ties all stacked in nice square stacks, they winched the mill back up that steep slope and told John Seivers they were ready for their pay. Seivers could not believe they had finished so quickly, so he went to see. He asked, "How am I going to get my ties out of there?" Brown told him that was his problem. Because of Arkansas ingenuity, John Seivers had to build his road after all.[115]

After the Sarvis Creek Lumber Company ceased operations, someone had started to haul a large boiler from the mill a few miles up Sarvis Creek.[116] The teamsters had only covered a short distance when their wagon upset and the boiler rolled down a particularly steep bank below the road. The boiler was then abandoned.

After that large tank had lain there a few years, H.E. Moore was able to buy it very cheap. Moore took his heaviest lumber wagon with the horses Chub and Pet as wheel team and Nig and Jeff as leaders. Cecil Long drove the four-horse team, and Moore followed with a smaller wagon loaded with camping equipment and all the chains, jacks, saws, shovels and other tools. There were two other men with them. They got to the boiler shortly after noon and spent the next several hours getting in position to roll it up that steep bank. Moore said it was about thirty feet almost straight up. The boiler was about twenty feet long and six feet in diameter. It was perfectly round, which helped a great deal. (It was the only boiler that Francis Moore ever saw that did not have a steam dome.) After getting the chains in place for a rolling hitch to bring the boiler up out of its nest, they put four horses on it with no luck before adding six—even less success. The horses would not pull together; they would each lunge forward then fly back. It was almost dark, and the boiler was right where they had first seen it. The men were quite discouraged, and while they were eating supper, Long said, "You know if Chub and Jeff were together and pulled like I have seen them, they would roll that boiler out of there by themselves."

Moore contended, "They wouldn't work as a team now, they haven't worked together for four years."

Since no one had a better solution, when morning came, the men decided to try it. With the chains already in place, Long said, "I just hooked Chub and Jeff on and told them, 'All right boys, it's up to you.' They leaned into it just as they had four years ago, with their chests only inches from the ground and scratching dirt as the boiler began to roll up those chains and in a matter of minutes it was laying in the road."

That had worked so well the men reset the chains and rolled the boiler on up the hill above the road so all they needed was to put skids underneath to load that boiler onto the wagon. Cecil Long remarked, "That just proves that a horse has a better memory than lots of people."

H.E. Moore used that old boiler for many years until he finally quit the sawmill business. He then let Ira Mason have it for scrap iron. Mason cut it into pieces and hauled it to Denver. He found the most valuable part of that boiler was the flues, thirty-six two-and-a-half-inch flues, twenty feet long. Mason cut the flue pipes in half to haul them and then advertised them as clothesline posts for one dollar each. People started flocking to buy them, so he raised the price to three dollars—still they still came. Moore said that Mason almost cried when he ran out of flues.

Irvin Shorter (Irv for short) came from Michigan with his wife and three children, two boys and a girl.[117] He worked for H.E. Moore off and on but also cut a lot of mine props on his own. Shorter and Moore decided if they could get the railroad to build a spur on the Laughlin property, it would solve a big problem, since team and wagon was the only transportation. Irv Shorter did all the legwork and filled out all the blanks and such. Finally, the railroad said that if Moore and Shorter would furnish the ties, the railroad would put in the siding. Since Shorter's name was on all the papers Shorter was the name given to the spur. Over the years, it was used a great deal;

H.E. Moore's last mill at Shorter's Siding, circa 1940. *Herold family collection.*

many carloads of lumber, props, ties and telephone poles were shipped by rail from Shorter's Siding.

Old Bill (William) Anderson drank fairly heavily (according to H.E. Moore). He and his brother-in-law, Lacy, would saw just enough lumber to get money to go down to town for a jug of whiskey. They would drink that and then go back to the timber to saw just a few more logs to get another jug.

Once when "Old" Bill Anderson was working as a sawyer for H.E. Moore at a mill on Greenridge, H.E. had a full crew ready to run the mill and a contract to fill on time; Bill was drunk and could not run the saw. When he was sober, Bill was a good sawyer, although he did have to stop between each cut to figure out the width of the next cut.

Running a saw was an art; it was the most respected and highest paid job in the mill. The sawyer had to look at the log, decide how wide to cut each board to get the most lumber from each tree. When setting the saw, it was up to the sawyer to figure out where the saw was to be set. After the first cut, the sawyer had to figure out how wide the kerf cut was, so that amount could be added to the setting for the next board, otherwise the board would be narrow and would not meet standards for the contract.

H.E. looked at Bill Anderson's son, "Young Bill," and asked him if he could run the saw. Young Bill kind of shrugged and said that he "could probably run it." H.E. told him to go ahead and saw the logs. That was

*the first time that "Young Bill" had worked by himself as a sawyer. He
was 15 or 16 years old at the time.*

*George Hogan was firing the boiler and helping another man as off
bearer (carrying the freshly cut boards to a pile and stacking them). Young
Bill was a "whiz" at math; he could figure the correct distances to advance
the saw without any wait between the cuts. After the mill had been running
for a while, George Hogan hollered at H.E. "Take that kid off that saw,
he's going to kill all of us." Young Bill was turning out lumber so fast that
the men could not keep up with the carrying and stacking.*

*Young Bill became known as one of the best sawyers around the Yampa
area. He could "squeak out" more boards from a tree than the scaling stick
said the logs contained.*[118]

When using any of the hand saws, crosscut saws or double crosscut saws,
any person who worked in the timber carried a small bottle of kerosene
around in his pocket.[119] The kerosene was poured in small amounts onto the
blade of the saw to cut the tree sap so the blade did not stick when they were
sawing down the tree.

Two French Canadians worked for H.E. Moore in the timber for a while.
Francis Moore said that he never did know any names for them other than
"Roy" and "Frenchie."[120] Roy was quite patient with Francis and showed
him some of the tricks for using a cant hook and other tools. One day, Roy

Stacks of sawn lumber waiting to be loaded onto trucks. *Courtesy of Yampa-Egeria Museum,
Fogg Collection.*

Unidentified men with a two-man crosscut saw. *Courtesy of Yampa-Egeria Museum, Fogg Collection.*

rolled a log down to the saw by jumping up on the log and rolling it down with his feet. For some reason, that struck Wylie Tomlinson as funny. That was the only time Francis ever remembered Tomlinson laughing out loud.

Sid Wheeler worked in the timber when Herb Moore's sawmill was up on Lawson Creek.[121] Wheeler always made sure that he got to the cook shack before anyone else could get there. He would sit down and start "shoveling it in" before some of the fellows could even get to the cookhouse. Wheeler would then get up and leave before anyone else was close to being finished with their meal. Rassy Chapman was the cook at the time, and he finally said that no one was to come to the cook shack until he rang the bell. Sid Wheeler still got there in a hurry. One day, he was sitting in the back of the long table that was fastened to the wall at one end. He had finished eating, so he started to crawl out under the table. Wheeler was in as big a hurry to leave as he was to arrive. Chapman met him with a butcher knife held under his nose and told him to "go and sit back down until everyone else is ready to leave." Sid sat back down—he was not going to argue with that knife.

One winter, Francis Moore was at the sawmill on Lawson Creek.[122] Sid Wheeler went into the cookhouse before the cook (this was a different year and a different cook from the earlier story) was ready for the men and sit down. He would eat anything that had already been placed on the table. This bothered the cook, so she made a rule that the men were not to go into the dining area until she was ready for them. She rang a bell (old round saw blade hanging on the porch of the cookhouse) five or ten minutes before the meal was ready so the men would have time to wash up before eating. Wheeler actually slept in the farthest bunkhouse, but he would sit on the porch of the closest bunkhouse with his hands on his knees, leaning forward, just waiting for that bell to ring. He would then make a big run for the washbasin so he would be the first person to the table. One of the fellows tried to slip a rope around his foot and planned to tie it to the bed. Another of the men made the comment that Sid would have "broke the rope" if he had actually been caught.

This is a story that Herb Moore related:[123] William Nelson was working in the timber with several others, including Herb. Nelson had notched a tree to fall in a certain way, but the tree did not go where he had hoped. It fell toward Sid Wheeler and almost hit him. Wheeler grabbed up his axe and started toward Nelson, cussing and swinging, saying that he was going to kill him. Nelson quickly started repeating, "It was an accident. It was an accident. It was an accident." Wheeler must have finally believed him, because Nelson was around for a long time after that.

Francis Moore recalled that Sid Wheeler was excellent at sharpening crosscut saws. He would sharpen them well enough that long ribbons of wood would fall from the kerf, not just pieces of sawdust. This skill was admired and sought after when those big crosscut saws were in use.

Wheeler and George Strickland were both doing contract timber cutting for H.E. Moore when they got into a quarrel over whose pile of logs belonged to whom.[124] H.E. came past on a sled, and they wanted him to settle the argument. Strickland was standing on the lower side of the sled; Wheeler was on slightly higher ground. When Wheeler got excited over anything, he did not want to argue, he wanted to fight. H.E. said he thought that Strickland could see that Wheeler was starting a fight. Then Wheeler hauled off and hit Strickland in the chin. Even though Strickland was standing in soft snow, the blow did not faze him in the least; he just asked Wheeler, "What are you trying to do?" Wheeler whirled around and stamped off down the road.

Sid Wheeler did not like to talk while he was eating; he said that eating was business, not a time to talk.[125] When he was working out in the timber, he would take a full ten-pound lard pail with his lunch and stop three times during the day to eat. This, of course, did not include his breakfast or supper, which he would eat before and after he went to cut logs.

Sometimes the cooks for the sawmills were men, but more common in the Egeria Park area, the cook was one of the men's wives. The families lived in small cabins; the children were often younger than school age. After the children got older, the wives would usually stay closer to town. Evelyn Pidcock recalled the Greenridge School, located on the northeast corner of Parker Brown's place, had students of both homesteaders and lumberjacks.

The barn on the Brown place (Brown's homestead on Greenridge) was hand-hewn by a man called Black Joe.[126] He was an Austrian. Francis Moore did not know his full name or where he got his nickname. Black Joe went without shoes all summer long; when he was hewing a log, he would put his foot on top of the log as a guide for his axe. He was extremely accurate with the axe and still had all his toes. He did not bathe during the summer, so the pitch and dirt built up on his feet to form a "sole" and probably was also some protection from the pine needles and rocks. He did wear shoes during the winter to keep his feet warm.

A man by the name of Garner had a sawmill in a small valley south of Whipple Park and north of Mill Creek. This is the location designated as the "slab pile" by the Moore family because of the strips and pieces of boards remaining at that site. Garner hauled the lumber to Steamboat. To get off Greenridge, he traveled down Raspberry Creek to the Yellow Jacket Road. (During a school field trip to Greenridge on September 22, 1999, Cecil Conner accompanied the fifth and eighth grades. He dated the Garner mill as being in existence in 1925, because in the past he had found several bottles in the sawdust pile as having that date.)

Charley Easterly excelled at sharpening saws. When Herb Moore was cutting telephone poles, he had "quite a bunch" of people working to cut the trees down. Easterly was hired to spend the day sharpening saws; the men would bring their saws to him to sharpen, and they would go back to cutting poles.

James Whaley had a sawmill that he moved to different locations on Greenridge.[127] It was a small mill, and Whaley could move it to the location of the timber. One of the locations was in what the Moore family calls the Buckhorn Camp. This is about half a mile northwest of the location for the Geer mill. In his interview with Carol Villa, Blaine Whaley stated that his dad also had a mill located in Wheeler Basin.[128]

Blaine was working with his father when he got his pant leg caught in the drive shaft that ran between the engine and the saw. Blaine hurt his leg and had a broken arm. "But, by spring I was fine," he declared.

At various times, Smokey Harris worked for H.E. Moore at different sawmill locations on Greenridge. But Smokey also ran sawmills of his own. He had a sawmill that was located at the top of Greenridge just west of Lawson Creek and north of the reservoir in Bison Park. This was probably the last mill to be located on Greenridge; it would have been running in the late 1940s. Smokey had gotten an old used boiler from somewhere. It was in poor shape and leaked "like a sieve." Smokey asked (Young) Bill Anderson to look at the boiler to see if he thought it would work. Bill said that he thought it would be okay as long as Smokey did not let the pressure get any higher than about 110 pounds.

Bill came back a few days later to see how the engine and boiler were working. Bill said that Smokey was running that boiler at 150 pounds of pressure—steam was leaking out of all the joints! Bill just turned around and left as quickly as possible. [This boiler evidently never blew up, because the author talked to Smokey in Kremmling, Colorado, about twenty-five years after that and he was in good shape.]

Before Smokey Harris worked in Bison Park, he had his mill located much closer to the top of Greenridge at the very headwaters of Lawson Creek. He ran out of water at this location and moved down into the park. Not long after Harris moved to the park, the land around the mill area became soft and marshy. He made the comment that "it is either drought or drown, I can't find the middle."

The last sawmill that H.E. Moore ran was located at the base of Greenridge at Shorter's Siding (just east of Colorado 131, at the junction of Routt County Road 21A). That mill ran for several years; the logs were brought down off Greenridge at different times with either horses or trucks. One of the more unusual methods of skidding in the Yampa area was the use of Francis Moore's crawler tractor. Both Francis and his nephew John Moore used it for pulling the logs off Greenridge. During the early 1940s, Irvin Shorter ran that mill for H.E. Two other sawyers were Bill Anderson and Bud Huffman. Mac Ogden also skidded and hauled logs during the 1940s. That mill burned in 1947 or 1948.

Bill Ragland had a mill at Trappers Siding (just south of Finger Rock).[129] He hauled the logs from Five Pine Mesa for that mill, which ran during the Depression era.

Fred Mohr recalled working at Ragland's sawmill during the Depression (possibly 1933).[130] Mohr used his own team to haul logs to the mill at Trappers Siding. Finally, the mill had to close during the winter because

Crawler tractor pulling a load of logs to the mill at Shorter's siding, circa 1940. *Herold family collection.*

of the deep, heavy snows; Mohr could not keep the sled from turning over on the way to the mill. He said that he spent most of his time loading and unloading the logs.

Bill Blakeman ran a planing mill north of Steamboat Springs. He moved the mill into Phippsburg during the 1940s and 1950s. At that time, it was one of the few mills in the area where the women worked alongside the men. One of the women was his daughter, Frances. Another was Garnet Railsback. Over the years, some of the local men who worked for Blakeman included Blakeman's sons, Lloyd and Bill Blakeman; the Railsbacks; Carl Herold; Wesley Moore; Roy and Roger Morgan.

The "bottom row" of graves in the Yampa Cemetery was where the county buried those who had no family in the area or those whose families could not afford a funeral.[131] Most of those graves had no stones or markers. One person buried there was Frank Bretz. Bretz worked for H.E. Moore in the timber as a sawyer for at least one year (around 1915). H.E. said that Bretz always stepped behind a tree when he felled it. H.E. had the habit of always stepping to one side when a tree fell in case the tree jumped straight back when it hit the ground or another tree. (This was called a kick-back.)

Once when Bretz felled the tree, the tree hit another tree with a large dead branch. That branch broke off and flew straight down to hit him in the forehead. The *Yampa Leader* included the following about the incident:

> *Last Friday afternoon while sawing down timber near the Moore sawmill on Lawson creek Frank Bretz, a timberman who has been working for Mr. Moore for some time was struck by a falling limb and rendered unconscious. Bretz and Moore were working together when a limb about two feet long and five inches in diameter broke from the top of the tree. Bretz attempted to get from under, but failing to do so the limb struck him on the head, fracturing his skull. Mr. Moore at once got assistance and the injured man was taken to the Yampa hospital and on examination it was found that his left side was completely paralyzed. He did not regain consciousness and died Saturday evening at 9 o'clock. A brother of the deceased was communicated with, who requested to have the deceased buried here. The deceased came here from Grand Junction last fall and was a hard working industrious man.*

In the mid-1950s, a fellow by the name of John Edmonton came to the Yampa area.[132] He was taking the logs that had been beetle killed and shipping them out of Yampa on the railroad. He was loading his trucks near Lower Stillwater, about where Coal Creek runs into Bear River. He hauled the logs down the River Road to Yampa with trucks. The town board of Yampa told him that he was not to haul anything wider than eight feet through the town, as it was too dangerous to have the trucks go through town with logs sticking out on each side of the trucks. Edmonton was cutting the logs into eight-foot lengths and stacking them into the trucks crossways. If the logs were not evenly stacked, the loads would be over the eight feet wide. Edmonton decided that he needed a backstop so the logs could butt up against it. This would even up the piles so they could then be loaded onto the trucks. Edmonton wanted a metal plate for the backstop, but he could not weld the metal sheets. Wesley Moore was working for Edmonton at the time as a sawyer and as a "choke chain" carrier. Wesley told Edmonton that he thought his dad, Francis, could weld it, even though it was heavy plate iron. Edmonton said to send Francis up and he could try.

Francis said that it was "wonderful welding"—all new metal and not old or "scrap iron" such as he was used to working on. He said that he did get kind of "lucky." He had tried to weld about an inch, and it was not sticking very well, so Edmonton asked Francis what he needed. Francis replied that he needed "more heat," so Edmonton increased the amperage on the welder. Francis then went ahead and finished welding the sheets for the backstop.

Edmonton declared, "You have been in the navy." He meant that Francis must have had formal training since he did such a good job of welding.

Francis replied, "No, I read a book or two, I'm just an old farmer."

The Maijala family first came into the Yampa area in 1944.[133] There were several brothers: Art, Reno, Raino and Ernie, plus others. Their first sawmill was located seventeen miles southwest of Yampa. In 1949, they moved their sawmill to Yampa—where they already had a planing mill—across the highway and railroad tracks from the east end of Moffat Avenue. In 1951, the Maijala family built a larger planing mill. The family not only sawed pine and spruce to sell locally in a family owned lumberyard, but they also shipped pulpwood out on the railroad. This pulp was mostly "quaker" (aspen) logs that were peeled.

Another Maijala family member mentioned that in 1943 when the timber supply was getting short in Vena, Minnesota, the Maijala family moved their lumbering operation to the Yampa area.[134] The equipment was shipped by train and then hauled by truck to the Gardner Park area. Small cabins were built to house everyone. Logs were skidded by horses to the mill and cut into lumber. The lumber was then hauled into Yampa, where it was sold locally or else sent out by train to the outside market. When the mill burned, including most of the housing, they moved into the Royal Hotel in Yampa and set up a new mill just east of town. This business was known as the Colorado Spruce Company and remained in full production for a couple decades.

There were several sawmills in upper Egeria (the area around Toponas); Dan Ray probably started the earliest one.[135] In 1921, Daniel Ray moved to South Routt County from Calico Rock, Arkansas.[136] In 1922, his first sawmill, the Ray Lumber and Sawmill Company, was established on King Mountain. In 1924, he leased land from William W. Reed in Toponas and engaged in the sawmill business from that location. It is thought that J.A. Aspegren, a Lincoln, Nebraska businessman, financed Daniel Ray's move to Colorado. When Daniel died in April 1926, Lily Ray did not know anything about the business arrangement between her husband and Aspegren; therefore, Aspegren leased the land and business operation from William Reed in Toponas and Mr. Ray's wife and children moved. Aspegren owned the business from 1926 until 1939, when Frank "Shorty" Strutzel bought it.

Frank "Shorty" Strutzel was born on April 12, 1894, in Dren, Austria.[137] He came to the United States when he was sixteen years old. Shorty worked

Right: Unknown couple sitting on a planed lumber stack at the Maijala's planing mill in Yampa, 1929. *Herold family collection.*

Below: Maijala's lumber yard, photo 2013. *Author's collection.*

in a sawmill on King Mountain in 1917 but entered the First World War and did not return to the sawmill business until 1931. He set up his first mill on Conger Mesa east of McCoy. In 1934, he and his family moved their sawmill back to King Mountain. The Strutzel family lived at the sawmill site on King Mountain until their daughter, Pat, reached school age. At that time, Shorty moved his base of operation to Toponas. During the 1940s, houses for the employees were added as they were needed. They were wired for electricity in 1943, and running water was added into the main house in 1946.

Shorty sold his lumber to Wenburg Lumber Company in Wisconsin and later to Straight Lumber Company in Denver, Colorado.[138] In 1951, Shorty Strutzel had sawmills in three different locations: on Five Pine Mesa, in Toponas and up Gore Pass not far from Rock Creek.

Some of the people who worked with or for Shorty Strutzel's mills include George Schultz, Frank Hart, Charlie Weaver, Matt Oliphant, Gay Bakke,

Lena or Lilly Schultz, Evelyn Overholt and Pat Strutzel standing by stacked ties at the sawmill on King Mountain. *Courtesy of Pat (Strutzel) Woodcock.*

Frank (Shorty) Strutzel loading a truck with mine props, circa 1938. *Courtesy of Pat (Strutzel) Woodcock.*

Jim Woodcock, Pat (Strutzel) Woodcock, Karen Craig and Jan Ray standing in front of the cookhouse for the Strutzel mill 2005. *Author's collection.*

James Ball, Pat Bratton, Kenneth Kirby, Chet Sanders, Tom Treat, Francis Moore, Wesley Moore and Wes Woodcock.[139] Shorty ran the sawmill at Toponas until 1975, when the last logs were cut. The planning mill was torn down in 1981 or 1982.

Dick Webb operated a sawmill on King Mountain.[140] Earl Ray (son of Daniel Ray) started working for Webb in 1930. They worked west of Harpers, up Egeria Creek. At some point, Webb moved to Toponas. They piled logs in the summer and sawed and planed them in the winter. Webb sold to the Lindas Lumber Company in 1946, and Earl Ray worked there until 1949, when Lindas died and the corporation broke up. Dick Webb loaned Earl Ray the money to buy the sawmill operation in Toponas in December 1949, and Ray ran the sawmill and timber operation until June 1968.

Some of Earl Ray's employers included Howard Kirby; Irvin, Richard and Herbert Ramsey; Anthony Treat; Hubbard Treat; and Wayne Ray (Earl's son).[141]

Simp Curtis ran sawmills in Upper Egeria; he had at least one on the Morrison Creek side of Greenridge.[142] Curtis's last mill was located south of the Toponas schoolhouse "just under the hill" overlooking Egeria Creek.

Railroad car of lumber from the Strutzel mill waiting to go to Denver. *Courtesy of Pat (Strutzel) Woodcock.*

That mill was still sawing timber in the early 1950s, but it burned in 1957. After the mill burned, Curtis and his family used their trucks to haul for other mills in the area.

In 1952, the Earl Jones family moved from Phippsburg to Lynx Pass, where they had two locations. They were on Lynx Pass until 1955.[143] They moved to a site on Highway 134 about six miles east of Toponas. That sawmill run by the Jones family was the last working sawmill in the Toponas area. Most of the logs for this mill were trucked from the Spruce Divide and Gore areas.

Although most of the sawmills in the Egeria Park area were small, family-owned mills, the timber industry had a large impact on the valley. Many farmers and ranchers worked in the timber to supplement their income. Others worked full time in the mills to support their families. Still others came into the Egeria Park area in the summer and went home to their families in Arkansas or elsewhere during the winter. Lumber from these mills was not only used locally but also sent to many different locations. Some went to buildings in Routt County, but different products were sent to places such as Denver and Chicago. Both trucks and railroad cars were used to ship the different forest products.

6

CATTLE AND SHEEP

When we think of open range, we usually picture the cattle running on the plains of Texas, New Mexico or eastern Colorado. Cattle were in those places, but they were here also. We do not think about South Routt County as open range, but for a few years in the late 1870s and the 1880s, there were almost no fences in the entire Yampa Valley.

When the valley was first settled, several cattle companies brought their cattle into the Egeria Park area, both from the Craig and Hayden areas in the western end of the county and from the Eagle Valley, coming through the Sunny Side area or over Red Dirt Divide. The idea was to summer the cattle here and then move them down to lower elevations for the winter. This removed the need for hay.

Some of the early settlers of the valley ran their cattle in Burns Hole during the winter. James Crawford "never ran more than two or three hundred cows," but he was one of the first to push the animals from the Yampa Valley over to the Burns Hole country.[144] He also was the first to settle in Steamboat Springs.

One of the larger cattle companies that ran its cattle in Upper Egeria was Coberly Brothers (William D. and Joseph G. Coberly). These fellows sent in six hundred head of Texas longhorns in 1879.[145] John Gibson and J.W. Whipple built the cabins and corrals in what is still called Coberly Gulch, a small valley on the west side of Spruce Divide overlooking Upper Egeria.

The Two-Bar Outfit, owned by Ora Haley, was one of the larger cattle companies in northwestern Colorado. Other names from that time include

Corrigan, the Cary Brothers, Clayton and Murnan, the Leavenworth Cattle Company, Pierce and Reef and the Snake River Pool. The headquarters for most of those ranches was in what is now Moffat County. There were few homesteaders, and the grazing was good enough that some of those large cattle ranches were able to stay in business until well after 1900. Those outfits wintered their cattle west of Craig and into Brown's Park. Some of them also wintered south toward the White River, Rangely and the Utah border. During the summer, the cattle were pushed up the various valleys to graze. During the 1880s, cattle from these companies could be seen along the Snake River, up Williams Fork, around Hayden, in Twenty Mile Park and Deer Park, even as far as the Egeria Park area.

Cattle and the cattle companies were important to the whole region. The anniversary edition of the *Pilot* quoted the following praises from the past.

"The luxuriant grasses and vegetation that grow in Routt County made this an ideal place to raise cattle....In the early days, vast herds fed in the Yampa and Snake River valleys, in Egeria Park and Burn's Hole."[146]

For a short time, both the early homesteaders and the cattle companies were claiming the grass here in the Yampa Valley. Some of the cowboys who rode for the cattle companies as young men brought their families into the valley later. Many of the riders for the large companies were the sons of the homesteaders or small ranchers in the area.

In Egeria Park, the homesteading and the open range occurred at almost the same time. This led to a certain amount of conflict between the homesteaders and the large cattle companies. One incident occurred when the Crossan family returned home in their wagon after visiting a neighbor.[147] Shaylor, a rider for the Corrigan Cattle Company, rode up to them and shot their dog. The dog did chase cattle at times, but on this particular day, he did not. Charges were brought against Shaylor, but the case was settled out of court. Not long after this confrontation, the Corrigan Cattle Company left the area.

Cattle with Yampa and the Laughlin Buttes in background, circa 1900. *Herold family collection.*

Riders moving cattle just south of Yampa, circa 1900. *Herold family collection.*

Some of the early settlers in the Egeria Park area who raised beef included the Birds, the Grays, the Wilsons, the Laughlins, the Choates and the Crossans. Evidently, some years they would have enough hay to feed their cattle at home; other years they would move them down toward the Grand River (Colorado River) or the Burns Hole area. Many of these early homesteaders retained cattle herds up through the early 1900s. Within a few years after they first came into the valley, they were joined by other cattle ranchers such as Jim Norvell, the Arnold Powel family and the Perry family.

Many of the early homesteaders had only a few head of cattle, and the loss of just one or two animals could make a great difference. Without necessarily meaning to, the large companies could gather homesteaders' cattle into the large herds that were wintered in the lower areas. The early homesteaders in South Routt banded together and formed their own cattle company. This allowed them to compete with some of the larger "cattle barons" that were using the valley for summer range. Some of the young sons of the homesteaders (the Gray and Bird boys for example) kept track of the cattle for the homesteaders. At other times, these same young fellows rode for the large cattle ranchers.

The *Steamboat Pilot* proclaimed, "The Yampa Livestock and Land Company was organized in 1882. Cattle were driven overland by Gore Pass until 1888, when the Denver & Rio Grande Railroad reached Wolcott."[148]

Even though the *Pilot* lists it as such, that cattle company would not have been the one in South Routt County. In 1882, what is now known as Yampa was still being called Egeria. What is now Craig was known as Yampa. The name Craig came into being in 1886; the town of Egeria then started calling itself Yampa.

Tom Laughlin did mention that at different times the early homesteaders ran their cattle together. They had a loosely formed Egeria Livestock Association. Loren Bird and Lowell Wilson were among the range riders for the Egeria area ranchers. Wilson rode some of the Greenridge and Morrison Creek areas; Bird rode some of the area toward the Little Flattops.

Even after the railroad arrived at Wolcott, not all of the people used its services. It was cheaper to let the cows walk on their own feet to the cattle buyer. Amazingly, about 1905, there was a better price for the cattle in Texas than in the northern states. Some of the stock from the Toponas and Burns areas were driven to Salida and loaded onto trains there. To get these cattle across the treacherous Colorado River, the cowboys had to be sure that the water was low enough to ford. The ford was evidently about half a mile below State Bridge. "Doc" Marshall was involved in some of those cattle drives.[149]

"Doc" and another young man were gathering cattle one fall over on Sunnyside near Dome Peak. These two fellows were working for one of the large cattle companies and were gathering all the cattle they could find. After they had been gathered, the cattle would then be split into bunches for the cattle owners. Some belonged to the large cattle companies, [and] some were owned by the local ranchers. The two cowboys were staying with an old Frenchman and putting each day's gather into his pasture until they had scoured the whole area before driving them all home. They were not taking a lunch with them for noon but going back about 4:30 or 5:00 hungry as wolves. "Frenchy" would then serve the best big fat juicy steak they had ever eaten. "Doc" said, "You could cut it with your fork." They were really enjoying the meat, as well as large servings of potatoes and gravy. About the third day of gathering, they all arrived back at the cabin at the same time, so "Doc" told "Frenchy," "You get the fire going; we will bring the meat." They went to a little shack down by the creek where they had seen "Frenchy" get those big juicy steaks. "Doc" said,

"We opened the door, and there it was—the hind leg of a horse, hoof and all! We went ahead and cut some steaks but, you know, they just did not taste so good after that, even though we knew it was the same meat we had thought so good only the day before. "Frenchy" told them it was a two-year-old filly that he had raised just to butcher. He said he loved horsemeat and butchered at least one each year.[150]

There are numerous records of cattle on those early homesteads. When they first arrived in the area, the Laughlin boys, Walter and Bennie, herded cattle while their older family members drove the wagons.

May (King) Wilson recalled that as the herds increased, the homesteaders pooled their cattle to run on the open range or else they just let them run together as they pushed them away from the plowed fields.[151] Tom Laughlin mentioned that he and one of the Birds were checking all the cattle out on the "alkali flats" (the sagebrush flats around the South Hunt Creek area) when his horse went lame. Whoever was with Tom was riding a horse he was just starting to train, and the horse could not be ridden double. That was the only time Tom remembered having to walk home. Another mention of pooling cattle was when Lowell Wilson was the range rider for the people who ran their cattle on Morrison Creek during the summer. He rode horses that belonged to the different ranchers.

These were small cattle owners—they did not have the thousands of cattle that the large cattle companies ran on the open range but ran their animals here at the same time as the large cattle companies. The end of open range in Egeria Park occurred before it did in other parts of the Yampa Valley. The fencing of the homestead fields stopped some of the free-ranging cattle. The large companies (Haley, the Carey brothers and others) kept the area open around Hayden and Craig for a longer period.

Tom Laughlin told of an incident in the early days at the Arnold Powell ranch. Arnold and his wife came from England and one of their former friends in England had a sixteen-year-old son, Reggie, who wanted very much to be a cowboy in the Western United States. All those Wild West stories he had read appealed to him. Therefore, Reggie's family offered Arnold a thousand dollars to keep the boy a year at the Powell ranch. They hoped he would get over his boyhood dreams.

Reggie arrived at the Powell ranch a couple days before spring branding. Uncle Tom said that Powell had many calves to brand and always called in all the neighbors to help. Since there were no branding chutes, it was

Feeding hay to the cattle. Mark Choate's ranch at the Sumner Buttes, circa 1905. *Courtesy of Yampa-Egeria Museum.*

always "rope, flank and hold"; Reggie was truly excited to be a part of a big branding crew. Arnold sent Reggie to the house, which was nearly a hundred yards from the corral, for some small item. Reggie jumped on Buck, an old cow horse that was handy and galloped to the house. On his way back, he thought he would show these western cowhands how a true English horseman rode. He spurred old Buck to a fast run and intended to jump the gate into the corral where they were branding. Just a few strides before they got to the gate, Reggie reared forward in the saddle and leaned far out over Buck's neck, as a true steeple chaser should. However, Buck had other ideas, he planted all four feet at the gate and stopped short! Reggie sailed over Buck's head and landed in the corral with a resounding splash of dust. Before the natives could comprehend what had happened, Reggie was on his feet and exclaimed, "Why, the bloody beast! He didn't take the leap." That really made the day for all the cowboys at the corral.[152]

A number of the ranchers in the area started improving the quality of their herds by adding purebred cattle. Some switched entirely to purebred animals. Shorthorns were brought in by some of the ranchers, including Mark Choate, in the early 1900s. But this area seemed to be better suited to

Herefords. Some of the names that come to mind include R.E. "Dick" Jones, Oat Perry and his son Junior Perry, Kenneth Hawkins, "Pat" Pastorus, W.P. "Wad" Hinman, Eddie Hinman, Kelly Klumker and Jack Reagor. Some of these fellows took animals to Denver in January each year to compete in the National Western Stock Show. A generous share of awards and ribbons came back to the Yampa Valley.

Jack Reagor was one cattleman who changed from the Herefords to high-quality registered Angus cattle. The Klumker family at Toponas introduced polled Herefords into their herd.

The cattle industry was, and still is, a major part of agriculture in Routt County. This can be seen in the fields and meadows filled with grazing cows as well as by visiting the county fair and watching the FFA and 4-H members show their animals. The South Routt animals have always placed well in the shows—not only in the Routt County Fair but also in the Colorado State Fair and the National Western Stock Show. Today, livestock are fed hay in the lower pastures and meadows during the winter months and put on pastures at higher elevations during the summer.

There were several reasons for the fights between the cattlemen and the sheep owners. The early stockmen, both cattle and sheep, had overgrazed

The Craig family's registered Herefords, just north of Phippsburg, 2011. *Author's collection.*

Moving cattle to the summer range, 2005. *Courtesy of Karen Craig.*

"Parade of Champions" at the Routt County Fair, about 1988. *Author's collection.*

the land, not realizing that the grasses in the arid West would not grow back as quickly as it did in the eastern United States. Until the 1890s, the majority of the sheep had ranged in Utah and Wyoming. Drought and overgrazing reduced the amount of forage in that area, so those herd owners were looking for new range. The cattlemen in northwest Colorado were also short of feed and were protecting their rangeland. Also, at that time, some cattlemen thought cattle would not eat grass after sheep had crossed the land. The cattlemen issued an ultimatum that the sheep were not to cross the Wyoming-Colorado line and enter the Colorado rangeland.

The disagreement over the range between sheep owners and cattle ranchers did not seem to affect the Egeria Park area as much as it did the Hayden, Craig and Meeker areas. Much of this was undoubtedly because the majority of the largest cattle ranchers resided in the lower valley. However, several prominent names from the Egeria area were in the Routt County Stockgrowers' association. Some of those same fellows went on the rides to the Wyoming line to stop the sheepmen. Those cattlemen included: Canant, Choat, Crossan, a couple of the Birds and the Grays. Some of the disagreements in the valley were handled in the courtroom; some were not.[153] The majority of the difficulties between the cattle and sheep owners seemed to have occurred during the thirty years between 1890 and 1920. In 1890 or '91, Johnny Wilkes brought sheep into the Battle Creek drainage.[154] It was stated that "hundreds" of sheep were killed or abandoned when Wilkes rushed back to safety in Wyoming. In 1894, there was another attempt to bring sheep into northwestern Colorado.[155] Representatives from the large cattle companies met Jack Edwards and his sheep at the state line between Colorado and Wyoming.

One contention between the cattlemen and the sheepmen came from the fact that the U.S. Forest Service had designated many of the permits on top of the Flattop Mountains as sheep range. For the sheep to get to this summer range, they had to travel across the traditional cattle ranges. Before this, the sheep from Wyoming had been trailed down the "sheep trail" along the Continental Divide, even to areas along the Rabbit Ears Pass. When traveling along this route, the sheep did not have to cross the lower valleys that were grazed by the large cattle herds.

A herd of sheep was clubbed and stopped at the Wyoming line by cowboys in 1911. From then until 1920, there was an outward appearance of truce. Again, the sheepmen tried to cross the traditional cattle ranges; the cowboys clubbed more sheep. Eventually, a sheepherder was also killed, bringing the fight over the rights of driving sheep across the pastureland into a court battle. The antagonism of both the sheep owners and the cattlemen was running so high at that time that the Colorado militia was brought into Craig, Colorado. To help settle the dispute, Farrington Carpenter of Hayden introduced the Taylor Grazing Act into Congress. The court decided which areas would have cattle permits and which areas would be for sheep. The court also decided where the sheep could cross the lower valley to get to their designated range.

One way that the sheep got to the Flattop permit areas was by traveling up the headwaters of the Yampa River southwest of the town of Yampa. Much of the area around Yampa had already been taken up in homesteads and had fences around the many fields. Also, some Egeria Park ranchers owned sheep. However, there were many cattle owners around Yampa who did not want sheep in the area.

Benson Male (a young man from a local family who helped a neighbor trail sheep to the Flattops) stated, "We worked hard to keep the sheep within the right-of-way fences and out of the meadows of the ranches on the sides of the road. Vestiges of the spirit that had sparked the very recent cattlemen's-sheepmen's range war still rankled in some of the ranchers, so we were careful not to cause offense."[156]

Sheep eat different types of grass and forbs than cattle do, so some of the ranchers in the area decided that sheep fit into the way the grass and hay could be utilized on their land.

Not too long after Francis and Gladys Moore were married, Gladys and her mother-in-law, Bertha Moore were fixing meals for a shearing crew [probably in the spring of 1933]. *At that time, the crew was shearing the sheep with the old hand shears. This meant that the crew stayed for several days and ate the noon meal with the sheep owners. This particular crew came in and sat down at the table and started eating whatever was already on the table (pickles, horseradish, etc.) Of course, the women would get the rest of the dinner on the table as soon as they could dish it up. Bertha (and all the rest of the Laughlins) used a lot of horseradish; it was their main meat relish. The first few days that the shearers were there, the horseradish was some that had been ground previously and was not too strong. This particular day, Gladys and Bertha had just ground fresh horseradish. The women had to laugh to themselves, when they came in carrying the rest of the meal. The shearers were busy eating the horseradish as the tears streamed down their faces.* [157]

In the early 1930s, hay and grain prices were quite low.[158] Herb Moore's solution was to get a small band of sheep and feed the hay and grain to them. There was always a cash market for sheep and wool. Herb heard that Fidele Lugon, who lived in Pleasant Valley south of Steamboat Springs, wanted to sell his sheep. Lugon wanted to vacation in a warmer climate out of the snow that winter. His sale price was fair, but he wanted all cash, which the Moores didn't have. Herb told Lugon, "We will buy your sheep and give you payments, spring and fall." Fidele hesitated until Herb pointed out that he would feed the sheep over the winter. In the spring, if he couldn't make the payment, Lugon could take the sheep back and he would still have his vacation. That sounded good to him, and he accepted the offer. Of course, Herb had every intention of making the payment and keeping the sheep.

A couple years later, the forest service let the Moores have a permit on the Flattops. It was called Dome Mountain permit, the first one over the rim to the south toward Dome Peak. The first year, Cass Peterson was the herder, and Foster Laughlin, Gordon Laughlin's son, helped drive the sheep up to the Flattops. With the help of two packhorses, Francis Moore moved the camp and set it up in its new location. It was probably the third of July when they topped over the rim of the Flattops and met a snowstorm from the north; luckily, they were turning south so their backs were to it. Francis told Peterson and Laughlin, "You bring the sheep; I will hurry on and set up camp." To get out of the wind and snow, Francis found a small hole about thirty feet across and about five feet deep. It seemed a perfect place for the camp, so he set up the tent as fast as possible and got a fire going. They spent the night there, but lo and behold, that hole turned out to be one of those basins that fill with water. The snow had turned to water and filled the small pond. Their bedding was soaked. Even though they had to move the camp to get it out of the water, that hole did give the sheep drinking water.

Cass Peterson was a sourdough artist. He knew the best way to keep a sourdough jug "working." [A person that used sourdough kept it in a crock and used some of it every day or two for the leavening agent in their breads, biscuits and hotcakes.] *Cass was very proud of his sourdough biscuits and pancakes. He delighted in serving them. His biscuits were almost as light as rolls and delicious when hot, but still very good when cold. For a sheepherder far removed from the nearest bakery, it was a good talent. But, when a person moved his camp that person had better use care when handling that sourdough jug. It was better to drop Cass's bed in the creek than to break the sourdough jug!*

The "bum lambs"
—bottle-fed orphan
lambs—about 1930.
Herold family collection.

When Francis Moore first got the sheep permit on the Flattops, the forest service banned open fires for the sheep camps.[159] Francis made a small stove out of sheet iron that could be carried on a packhorse. It had folding legs but was still awkward to get into the Flattops. Clyde Elgin was using a mare, Gyp, as a packhorse to get the food and supplies into the sheep camp. He balanced the pack and put that sheet-iron stove on the top of the load. Even though Gyp was a gentle horse, and considered a good packhorse, she caught sight of that stove out of the corner of her eye and started bucking. She bucked so hard that she managed to buck everything off. There was gear and supplies scattered over a wide area. That new stove carried the dents from landing on the rocks and ground all the years they took sheep to the forest permit.

The Moores summered the sheep on that permit for three years, which should have given them a permanent permit by the forest service's own rules, but they were cut off the fourth year. When they complained to the forest ranger, he said they had been running on another person's holdover, The Moores pointed out that a holdover lasts for only one year; the ranger then claimed it was a different person each year.

The Moore family never tried to investigate and change that decision because Dome Mountain was not a very good permit. One year, it was so wet the whole range got spongy, just like a swamp. It was so wet that even some of the lambs got foot rot (a bacterial disease carried in wet ground). Another year, it was so dry they had to take the sheep off an extremely steep slope to Island Lake for water each day and go back on top to graze. When there was enough rain to keep the sumps full of water, everything was wonderful—otherwise, it was a problem.

During the 1940s and early 1950s, Ray Kaufman, Leonard Ekstrom, Herb Hamilton and Francis Moore each had a band of sheep. (A band can range in number from about 1,000 ewes with their lambs to 1,200 ewes with their lambs.)[160] They hired a Mexican crew to come each spring and move from ranch to ranch to shear the sheep. Those crews were a complete unit of about thirty or more men. The shearing machines were all mounted on one truck, six clippers on each side. All they needed was a large pen, about thirty feet by thirty feet. They placed the truck in the center; then Francis Moore and his help would crowd about sixty or seventy sheep into that same pen. Each shearer would grab a woolly, shear it and then turn it loose in the same pen. When all were sheared, that group of sheep was rotated with more woollies. With so many shearers, rotations of shearers happened quite often. The shearing crew also tromped and bagged all the wool. With a crew this large, the shearers spent only one to one and a half days at each of the four ranches.

Those crews asked each rancher to keep the pen full of sheep. When they first arrived at the corral, they also asked each rancher for one dry ewe or wether for meat. (This was in addition to the normal shearing fees.) It would be the first sheep sheared. The cook would immediately grab, kill and dress it and have it cooking in a pit he had already prepared before the animal had hardly stopped kicking. The fire in that deep pit burned slowly, so by noon the meat and beans (or whatever else was cooking) were cooked completely.

Around noon, Francis Moore expected them to stop for lunch, but not so. There were enough of them that a young amateur would grab the clipper while the regular shearer went for lunch. Thus, the machine never stopped. So Francis and his helpers had to do likewise; one or two of them would go to lunch while the others stayed to keep the shearing pen full of sheep.

Sheep were shipped each fall, usually in September, circa 1945. *Courtesy of Yampa-Egeria Museum.*

The first year, Francis took a large ten-gallon can of nice fresh water and set it in the shade to keep it cool. Soon, he noticed the can was set in the sun, so he moved it back into the shade. Not long after that, it was again set in the sun—come to find out, they didn't want cold or even cool water. They had drunk warm water all their lives and liked it that way.

One of the first years that Francis Moore had sheep, the price for wool was not very high. He had his wool sacks stored in the shop to keep them dry, hoping the price would go up. One day, a "slick fellow" came by claiming to be a wool buyer. He looked at Francis's wool and told Francis that it was exceptional. He was sure he could get the top dollar in Denver and said he would take a sack out to the market. (A wool sack is a large burlap bag that holds numerous fleeces. When full, they weigh 175–300 pounds, depending on the amount of dirt and lanolin that is in the wool as well how tight the sack is tromped.) They made a deal. When the fellow loaded the one sack onto the pickup, he said that he might as well take three, as that is what would make a load on the pickup. They weighed the bags as they loaded them. He gave Francis a personal check for all three sacks, so Francis let him take them.

A few days later, Francis took the check into the bank to cash it, and there had been a "stop payment" put on the check. The man had tried to sell the sacks of wool to a wool broker in Denver and could not get as much as he had paid Francis. Francis went to Denver to talk to the so-called buyer. His address was just a small room on Larimer Street. There was no one at home. At the time, Francis Moore was dealing with the Oak Creek State Bank. (This bank later moved to Steamboat and became the Routt County National Bank.) Burt Cand and Albert Cruze were the officers of the bank at the time. Francis talked to Albert Cruze again. Albert talked to the bank in Idaho Springs, on which the check had been written. After that, Albert met the so-called wool buyer with the check in one hand and a warrant for his arrest in the other. Albert told the fellow that if the check went through the bank, the warrant would not be served. The check went through.

Francis had several more sacks of wool to sell that year. That was probably when he started working with Ray Kaufman, Leonard Ekstrom and Herb Hamilton to pool their wool together. When the four of them sold as a small wool pool, they would have a full railroad car of wool. This gave them a better bargaining position than any one of them had as a single seller.

One year (possibly just before World War II), the price of wool rose rapidly. Ray Kaufman usually did the dickering for the group. He followed the market and seemed to enjoy the bargaining. The fellows were all delighted when Ray called and said that the price was up to $1.00 a pound. Kaufman wanted to wait and see if it went any higher. They all agreed that would be all right. A couple days later, he called and said that the price had risen to $1.10. They all decided to take it, as they were afraid the bottom was going to go out of the market. The next time Kaufman called, he told Francis that they didn't have any wool, as he had sold it for $1.12 a pound. Everyone was quite happy with that price, even though the price had risen to $1.15 before the market for wool collapsed.

They did enjoy kidding Frank Stetson though. Stetson turned down $1.15 for his wool; he was holding out for $1.25 a pound. When the price dropped, he had to take less than a dollar a pound for his wool that year.

The little "Yampa Wool Pool" worked well for several years. This was possibly the inspiration for the Routt County Wool Pool that was formed a few years later. The wool from sheep that are wintered in Routt County is unique because it is much cleaner and higher quality than wool from sheep that are wintered in an area with little or no snow; the wool in those areas picks up dirt and sand from the wind and ground.

Francis Moore didn't remember the year, but Ray Kaufman found that there were winter permits available for several thousand sheep near Thompson, Utah.[161] Kaufman was very excited and bragged it up to all of them. He wanted them to take their herds to the winter range and then they would have no more pitching of hay on cold winter days. Not pitching hay on cold days did sound good, but moving the sheep to winter range didn't appeal to Francis, so he told them, "I know how to pitch hay, but don't know anything about winter range." Kaufman, Hamilton and Ekstrom all decided to go. They trucked their sheep down there for two winters. Both of those winters were dry ones, with no snow to furnish water for their sheep. That meant they had to haul water each day for most of the winter. There were other problems, such as having to buy troughs for the water. It did not work out as well as they had hoped, so after two years, they all went back to pitching hay. Francis noted, "My being cautious paid off that time."

About 1952, Francis turned down a super deal. He was looking for two hundred young ewes to add to their herd. A sheep salesman from South Dakota offered to take a man from Hayden and Francis to look at sheep. He would show them any number or age of sheep they wanted. It was the first time Francis had been to South Dakota, [and] *on the trip the salesman said repeatedly, "You guys ought to sell your ranches in this old snow bank and buy in the Dakotas, it's God's country." But when they got to Dakota all the sheep, young and old looked like they had been gutted* [lean, lank and skinny]. *Francis kept thinking, if the country is so good what's wrong with the sheep?*

The first day, the salesman took them to a ranch to show them some four and five year old ewes. They arrived at the corral just as the owners were bringing the sheep in. Francis and the other Routt County fellow jumped out of the car, thinking they would help steer them into the corral. The sheep not only looked like greyhounds, they ran like greyhounds, a man on foot didn't have a chance. The ranchers in Dakota herded with pickups and dogs; because the range was as flat as a table the pickups worked well. The man from Hayden topped 300 head out of the bunch at $9.00 a head. The owner then turned to Francis and said, "There are four hundred head left of this herd, granted a good many culls, but if you will buy them all, at $3.00 per head they are yours. I want to finish this bunch and let the herder go." As it turned out that was one of the best bargains Francis was ever offered. Nevertheless, he turned it down, thinking "If this country is so great, what is wrong with the sheep?"[162]

However, Francis did buy two hundred head of two-year-old ewes from another ranch, but he had to pay twelve dollars per head. Those ewes grew

A typical farm flock. This flock contains two different breeds, Suffolk and Columbia. *Herold family collection.*

The Willie Ranch's purebred Rambouillet flock in Deer Park, 2008. *Author's collection.*

all winter long; by spring, they looked like different sheep. Later, he talked with the Hayden man who said his older ewes did well also. They put on weight all winter.

You will no longer find large flocks of sheep in Egeria Park during the winter months. A few herds still graze on the Flattops during the summer but are moved to lower elevations during the winter. There are some farm flocks that remain in the area yea-around, and the FFA and 4-H kids still enjoy the sheep projects.

Cattle and sheep both utilized the pasture and hay in South Routt County from the time the first settlers came and continue to do so. The climate of the area is suited to the grazing of livestock. There aren't as many large ranches in the area as there once was, but you will still find a few cattle and sheep grazing in the mountain pastures. If you listen closely, you might hear the sheep bells ringing or cowboys hollering as livestock travels across the range.

SCHOOLS, POST OFFICES AND OTHER ESTABLISHMENTS

The nucleus of any new community revolves around the places where people gather to visit and exchange news; schools, post offices and stores have always served as gathering places. As one would expect, those enterprises in Egeria Park also served as community centers.

SCHOOLS

Schools have always been important to the South Routt area. A school district recognized by the county could be formed as soon as ten children could be included in the school. These schools, which contained grades one through eight, could be placed close enough to the homesteads so the young children could walk or ride to the school. Some schools had a barn where the students could stable their horses in bad weather. Others held school in the summer term so the students didn't have to travel in bad weather. After 1884, county superintendents held an elected position.

Quite often these superintendents were schoolteachers before they became superintendents. There was only one superintendent for the entire county, and he or she covered many miles throughout each school term. Before the counties were divided in 1911, the superintendents covered what is now both Moffat County and Routt County. He or she was expected to visit each school several times throughout the year. It was also his or her job to administer the county test to the eighth graders before those students could graduate. Emma Peck was the county superintendent from 1894 to 1896 then again between 1912 and 1920.

"Often called a 'pint size lady,' she was a buckboard-and sleigh-driving county superintendent, covering as high as 2,000 miles in a term through some of the West's most rugged country."[163]

These superintendents were well received and liked by the small country schools. Quite often, when these ladies or gentlemen came to a school, the students were asked to recite a current lesson or show an example of their penmanship. Sometimes a full program was presented. Their visit was not only important to the children but also considered a newsworthy item.

In 1905, "Miss Verna Bartz our popular school superintendent visited the [Egeria] school Wednesday. She was accompanied by Miss Eleanor McLaughlin of Steamboat."[164] The Bartz family lived in Steamboat Springs, and Verna graduated from high school there.

There were at least ten or eleven country schools in Egeria Park.[165] Some of the schools were held in homes or in empty cabins; the location of a school might move to be near the largest population of students. Many of these schools were open for only three months when the weather was good. Schools were built in locations where the students could walk or use horses. Some of the students would attend school for part of the semester, as they stayed home to help with the work. No wonder students were sometimes older than their teachers. May King Wilson recalled that at least three of her students were older than she was when she took her first teaching job (about 1893) at the Bear River School.[166] (Even though Wilson called this Bear River, it was also called the Upper Yampa, the Five Pine or the Lancaster school. The name depended on which location it was held; the students seemed to be from the same families, no matter which name was used.) This school was located on the Bear River southeast of Yampa.

The Rockhill School was located on the Rockhill ranch just west of the Devil's grave on William "Billy" Rockhill's homestead.[167] The only students were the Rockhill children. The next year, a cabin was built about a mile northwest on South Hunt Creek and included other children. This was naturally called the South Hunt Creek School. By 1919, this school had merged with the Heart Mountain School.[168]

The Heart Mountain School had at least three separate locations. In 1916 and 1917, Gladys (Margerum) Moore attended the Heart Mountain School when it was located "on the old road in the little hollow just west of what we used to call the Luckett Hill."[169] This would place the school on

Lancaster School, District 20. *Courtesy of Yampa-Egeria Museum, Alan Rice–W.W. Carle Collection.*

County Road 13, just east of where the road crosses South Hunt Creek. The Elmer Margerum (C.E. Margerum) homestead was located too far from a school for a six-year-old to walk, about four miles west. Gladys stayed with her maternal grandparents, the Hunicks, during the week; the Hunicks homesteaded the place that was a "short mile" west of the school. Gladys was able to walk to school for her first two grades.

The second location was north of the South Hunt Creek bridge on the Crosho Lake road. It must have been there only one or two years. The third and best-known location for the Heart Mountain School was on the Crosho Lake road (County Road 15) west of the bridge. At that location, the school served the area from 1919 until 1950.[170] Jack Redmond mentioned that the log school building was moved on skids from one location to the other.[171]

The Terhune Basin School, Lone Spring School and the Seyfang Ranch School were again different names for the same school. The location for this school changed from one ranch to another; the name changed as well.

The very first school in Egeria Park was held in Henry Crawford's cabin in 1883.[172] This cabin was evidently just south of the present Yampa cemetery and was known as Egeria School District No. 6. The first school directors were Alex Gray, Mark Choate and William Bird. The first teacher was John White. The next summer, a schoolhouse was built in the saddle of the hill

The second Watson Creek School, located on "upper" Watson Creek, District 20. *Herold family collection.*

just north of the cemetery. It was located on the "old road" where it goes out of sight behind what is now the shooting range. When the school was located there, it was also known as the Watson Creek School. Some years later, the school in District 20, located several miles southwest on upper Watson Creek, became known as the Watson Creek School.

After the district built a school within the town of Yampa, the school building near the cemetery was moved about halfway to Phippsburg. It served as a school at the Mark Choat homestead for a few years and moved again to a location just south of Phippsburg. The *Oak Creek Times* noted, "The Phippsburg School district voted to move the old Egeria School to Phippsburg in 1937."[173]

Tom Laughlin reminisced about that first school. Laughlin and all the other children in the area attended a three-month summer school.[174] At that time, it was the only school in Egeria Park, and for a few years, all children from Yampa, Phippsburg and their surrounding areas attended. As more children came of school age, more schools were built. It is amazing those students received as much education as they did. Francis Moore's mother, Bertha, was six years older than her brother, Tom. She had beautiful handwriting, was a good reader and read a lot. Francis commented, "She was no whiz at math, but at least she could take care of a checkbook."

One story about the Egeria School related that all the boys took their lunches up to the white sandstone rocks when they ate their noon meals. They would scratch their names into the sandstone (volcanic ash) with the idea that those carved names would last for many years to come. Since this was exceptionally soft stone, it soon deteriorated from erosion, and those early names only lasted six or eight years.

> *Those same boys told about Clyde Elgin, he was the son of George and Anne Elgin. Mrs. Elgin was a very good cook, and she sent good lunches with Clyde in a ten-pound lard pail; she always packed his sandwiches on the bottom and the things that would mash on top. Clyde would eat his lunch standing up with the pail tucked under his arm. Clyde never unpacked his lunch; he ate everything from top to bottom, if there was pie packed on top that was eaten first.*

Sometime before 1902, a one-room log school was built on what is now 236 Main Street in Yampa. This building has been renovated and is now a private residence. In 1903, a building boom occurred in Yampa in anticipation of the coming railroad. The little log school building quickly became too small for the numerous students. A one-story frame building was built on the corner of Third and Main Streets on what was to become "the school block." The ground was donated to the school district by Lewis Bird. The Birds' house and barns remained on that block until about 1916, when Lewis moved the buildings to a spot west of Finger Rock.

> *The children who lived in town walked to school from their houses. Some of the students that lived on nearby ranches rode their horses to town, then left their animals in a friends or relatives barn. Many homes, even houses in town had a barn. Some of the town houses had a well located in their yard. Those who did not, shared a "town well." At least one community well was located near the corner of Clifton and Second Street.*
>
> *One of the chores that many children were expected to complete was carrying a bucket of water after they got home from school at night. As might be expected there was many a snowball fight or mumblety-peg game carried out before the water got home for the night.*[175]

The next school was a white two-story frame building that was located where the present elementary school stands; a high school was added and met upstairs. Alfred Buck, Helen Crowner and Lila (Allen) Crossan were the

The first one-story school in Yampa, about 1909. *Herold family collection.*

first three students to graduate. The large cottonwood trees at the present school were planted in the schoolyard of that two-story building.

Yampa was the only high school in Egeria Park. Any of the students who had graduated from the eighth grade in the country schools came to Yampa to attend high school. Because the roads and winter weather made it impossible for students to travel great distances, many students boarded with someone who lived in town. At other times, one or both parents would move into town for the winter so the children could attend high school. Occasionally, other circumstances made it necessary for students to move into town to attend school.

In time, the two-story building became too small to house the students. Another one-story frame building was erected on the west side of the same block. By 1915, the first through third grades met in the smaller building.

Once again, the student population became too large for the existing buildings, and a two-story brick school was constructed. The students all moved into the new brick building after the Christmas break in January 1924. Several of the older students helped move the books and supplies from one building to the other during the holiday break.[176] In 1925, the two-story frame building was torn down, and the lumber was used to build two houses in the 200 block of Clifton Avenue. The one-story building was moved northwest of town to the Areola ranch. With additions, those buildings are still in use as private residences. In 1952, a one-story brick building was built for the high school in the same location as the frame school had occupied. The main entrance for this school faced Main Street.

Dan Trantham died when his three children—Martha, Alfred and Willard—were still quite young. Maude, his wife, moved into town and worked as a custodian for the school.[177]

Yampa School, with Maynard Burgess and Benson Male in the bell tower, about 1918. *Herold family collection.*

Willard Trantham was in the same classroom with Francis Moore when Mr. Baird came in to teach. The class needed to "catch up" on their learning. The students in the front of the class were to look towards the front of the room. They were not to look back at the other students. The teacher would throw a book at the back of the kid's heads if they turned around to visit with any of the other kids. Willard Trantham was in the back of the room, right next to the old wood stove. That stove had a metal protector around it. This metal sheet was several inches off the floor and extended about 4 feet up into the room, this deflected the heat so the students that sat next to the stove didn't get too hot. Francis didn't know what Willard did; perhaps talk to another kid, but whatever it was the teacher did not like it. The teacher threw a screwdriver down the aisle and hit that metal sheet that was in front of the stove. The terrific noise certainly "woke up" all the kids and made them pay attention to the teacher.

Some teachers in the one-room schools taught for only one or two years before getting married or else moving on to other jobs. But some teachers made a career of teaching. A few of the teachers that taught in the 1940s and on into the early 1950s include the following.

First through third grade, one-story building in Yampa, circa 1915. *Herold family collection.*

The two-story brick school in Yampa, 1925. *Herold family collection.*

Josephine Ray taught in one room schools and then started teaching in the McCoy school. Even after she retired, she could be persuaded to substitute in Yampa Elementary.

Lila Ault taught in McCoy and then moved to Yampa Elementary, where she taught the fifth and sixth grades for several years. She was a firm believer in discipline and the old-type curriculum. One of her ideas was that every student should learn penmanship. Every day after lunch, she read a chapter or so from a book while everyone dipped a straight pen into the ink and practiced the Spencerian way of writing. The books she chose were great; *Little Britches*, *Moby-Dick* and *Juan and Juanita* were a few that she shared with her students. However, her discipline did not meet with all the parents' approval. Some of the parents tried to get her fired, using the argument that she did not have "enough education" to be a teacher. The school board kept her, as the board felt she was one of the better teachers in the school.

Ann Crawford taught in the Toponas school for several years before the Toponas district joined Yampa. Crawford then taught for several more years in the Yampa Elementary.

Ilda (Margerum) Montgomery taught in several one-room schools throughout the area before she moved to the Yampa Elementary.

In small-town schools, outstanding sports teams seem to run in cycles. From 1913 to 1915, the boys in the Yampa schools were quite good at sports:

The football team did very well, winning most of their games. Some of the team members were Earle Moore, son of H.E. and Bertha Moore. Willard Brown, an exceptional athlete, who was also quite good at school work. Channing Reed, who lived up towards Toponas. Kenneth Ludkie, whose parents had a small place near Yampa; they later moved to Oak Creek and ran a drug store.

At that time, no one had their names written across the back of their jerseys. This bunch of boys wanted their name on their uniforms. They decided to paint their last names on the seat of their football pants, so when they bent over on the line the names could be read. When Earle printed the name Moore on his pants, the paint ran on the last two letters and looked like an "n." Thus, instead of "Moore," he became "Moon." Even after he got out of school, a lot of the people still called him "Moon," especially the people near his age group.

Not only was the football team quite good at this time, the boys did very well in track. They went to Steamboat for a regional track meet, and Willard came back with so many medals that he could hardly walk. Earle

Yampa High's boys' basketball team. *Left to right* (*top*): Bert Terhune, Ed McLaughlin, Melvin Burris and Walter E. Howe; (*bottom*) Carey Trantham, Art Orr, Francis Moore (captain), Mervin Montgomery and Elmer Alfred, 1927. *Herold family collection.*

Yampa High School girls' basketball team. *Left to right*: Ruby Ray (captain), Bertha Montgomery, Nell Francis, Thelma Margerum, Ione Trantham, Bernice Montgomery, Katherine Carnahan, Mildred Russell and Hazel Hoffman, 1930. *Courtesy of Hayne-Ray Collection.*

got a medal for the Hammer Throw. They only gave medals for first place at that time. The boys here in Yampa had never had a hammer so they could practice, so Earle didn't know how to throw it. He just picked it up by the handle with one hand and spun around a couple times and turned loose. The Steamboat Springs coach told him, "My gosh kid! If you had used two hands, you would have thrown it away."[178]

Francis Moore offered some insight into the school basketball program after he graduated in 1928:

About three or four years after I was out of school, the Yampa High School basketball team won the district championship and went to Denver for state contention and won second place, losing their final game by only one point. Mr. Gillet was the coach and during the fall and winter of that year, he appealed to some of us who were just out of school to come give the school team some competition. Five of us formed what we called a town team and played them several games that winter, most times they beat us, but when they won second in state, we were as proud as they were. We felt we had a part in their training.

The county school districts were reorganized in the fall of 1960; the schools of Yampa and Oak Creek were combined. The Yampa Bears and the Oak Creek Miners became the Soroco Rams, with the high school located in Oak Creek and the elementary in Yampa. The students were bused to the schools.

POST OFFICES

Getting mail into Egeria Park could be unpredictable until a regular stagecoach route was established. In the summertime, the horseback ride from one place to another was comparatively easy. Winter trails held many problems.

Z.B. Maudlin came to the area on September 12, 1879. Just seventeen days later, the Meeker Massacre occurred.[179] At that time, he was in Steamboat Springs with his partner Ed Hodges. After the Indian scare, they were looking after cattle belonging to Bert Smart. On January 1, snow began falling, and for eleven days they did not see the sun. It was so cold, they could hear their nearest neighbor, six miles down the canyon chopping wood. The following story was related in the newspaper in 1937 ("Rock Creek" is on Gore Pass):

> *Talk about your mail service, we had no Christmas presents that year. Relay carriers on snowshoes brought mail from Georgetown. The first relay post from Georgetown was Hot Sulphur Springs. Three carriers were used to relay between the two post offices. The next post office was Rock Creek. From Rock Creek, the carriers made it into Steamboat Springs. Hodges became postmaster at Hayden and for a while Z.B. Maudlin was carrier. He said he had fought the wind, and "I had 60 or 70 pounds of mail on my back when the thermometer was 35 degrees below zero. What do you suppose Uncle Sam paid me—$40 a month and I boarded myself."*

Maudlin said that one carrier between Rock Creek and Steamboat Springs failed to come in on schedule. A search party found him half buried in the snow. They hauled him on a hand sled twelve miles into Steamboat Springs. The snow was deep, they couldn't always control it and he rolled off a dozen times or more. When they got the mail carrier to Steamboat Springs, his feet were frozen. He lost all his toes except one and was laid up for the remainder of the winter.

In the winter, the mail carriers traveled from the Front Range over the Continental Divide into Hot Sulfur Springs, over Gore Pass and then on into Egeria Park. Three or four mail carriers would do this 150-mile route. Some of these men used skis, while others used snowshoes; at the time, the early residents referred to what we now know as skis by the name of Norwegian snowshoes or simply snowshoes. When one reads the old stories, one cannot be sure whether they were using skis or actual snowshoes. Sometimes these men would pull a trail sled behind them, or at times they carried a backpack with the mail. The following story occurred sometime between 1880 and 1885:

> *Just after the first settlers came to the Yampa Valley, the only mail in the wintertime came over Gore Pass. It was carried by a man on snow shoes. Someone in the area had ordered an accordion from a mail order house. The mailman not knowing what was in the package said no matter how many times he changed position or turned that mail sack, it just continued to dig holes in his back. Finally being exasperated with it, he just laid it on a stump and beat it with a club until it got soft. When they opened*

the mail sack at the first Post Office, all that was left of the accordion was some very small pieces mixed through the letters.[180] [One wonders if the person who ordered it said it was damaged in the mail and asked for a refund. Hopefully, he waited for summer before ordering another.]

The first post offices were in homestead cabins. That meant the homesteader or his wife accepted the job as postmaster; they then kept the mail in their own cabin.

The first Egeria Post Office was established at the E.H. (Ed) Watson ranch in 1883, with Watson serving as the postmaster.[181] If there was mail for anyone in Egeria Park, it was dropped into a box in the corner of his house. According to the stories, if Watson or his wife were not in their cabin when the owner of a letter came to pick it up, that person was welcome to go into the cabin and retrieve his own mail.

The Egeria Post Office was the only post office in the area. May (King) Wilson recalled going from their place south of Toponas to Yampa to get their mail.[182] (The Kings came into the Toponas area in 1884.) In the summer, the mail for Upper Egeria was left in a box at the "corner of the main road." In the winter, the mail had to be collected from the Egeria Post Office, which had been moved to the Elmer Hoag ranch. Elmer Hoag's cabin was about a quarter mile south of the Watsons' homestead. The post office seemed to move to whoever was willing to have it in their home. The official location was never changed by the postal department.[183] But the locations of the various postmasters cover a distance of about seven miles. The Elmer Hoag place and the Mark Choate cabin have both been mentioned in several of the older manuscripts as locations of the post office.

When the Newcomer family homesteaded in Upper Egeria, the mail for that area was left at their cabin.[184] Sam Reed's house also served as a post office for those early settlers in Upper Egeria. As more people came into Egeria Park, more post offices were established. By 1888, an official post office was established at Toponas with Levi Newcomer serving as the postmaster.[185]

The Yampa Post Office was officially established in 1894. By this time, the Egeria Post Office had moved to Herod Fulton's homestead north of what is now Phippsburg. With the establishment of the Yampa Post Office, Egeria Park had three post offices. People, who lived on King Mountain south of Toponas or those who lived west of Yampa near the flattops no longer had to ride twenty miles to pick up their mail.

The first Egeria Park Post Office was in Ed Watson's homestead cabin (*center*), circa 1890. *Herold family collection.*

The Yampa Post Office has had many different physical locations. Again, many of these changed with the postmasters. The first actual location was in the Fix Store, located on the west end of Moffat Avenue. The postmaster was Samuel Fix.

In 1901, Judge Warren Carle became postmaster. Sometime before 1906, a large two-story building was in place (next to Judge Carle's home on Main Street); the post office was located in a first-floor corner. Hugh McGaughey carried the mail from Yampa to Steamboat at that time.[186]

The *Yampa Leader* had this to say in 1903: "Judge Carle is having a plank walk put down in front of the post office."

The formality of the postal service in the area changed considerably between the time of Ed Watson's box in the corner of his cabin until the time when the following article in the newspaper was printed. In 1903, the people of Yampa may have considered themselves to be well past the "good old days": "Postmistress Lyons has made a change at the post office this week. She expects a lot of new lock boxes this week."[187]

The same paper had this to say about the mail delivery: "Sunday evening while the driver was getting out the mail at Yampa the Wolcott Stage horses took a header down the street. Harry Lampshire lost a few rods of fence, but no damage to the outfit. Must be feeding oats to the stage nags."[188]

The first post office in Yampa was at the west end of Moffat Avenue inside Sam Fix's store, circa 1903. *Herold family collection.*

Judge Carle built a two-story building on Main Street; the post office was on one side of the bottom floor, circa 1905. *Courtesy of Yampa-Egeria Museum.*

The Yampa saloon, on the corner of Moffat Avenue and Main Street, was turned to sit at an angle in the 1930s. It was the post office about 1950. *Author's collection.*

The post office seems to have been located in the same building when this article appeared in the 1908 newspaper. The two buildings mentioned in the article sat across Main Street from each other: "The post office building and the Buck and Moore's building are resplendent in new coats of paint."[189]

The location of the post office has changed several times since 1903; it moved back to the store originally owned by Sam Fix on the corner of Moffat Avenue. Later, it moved to the old saloon turned to a salon, on the corner of Moffat Avenue. For a time, it was located in a building on the south side of Moffat Avenue, directly across the street from the Royal Hotel. There was a move to the Royal Hotel on Moffat Avenue, and it is currently located in the brick building next to the former location of the Royal Hotel.

In Upper Egeria (the Toponas area) the post office also started in homestead cabins, and as in many of the other settlements of the area it was moved to the general store. It now occupies its own building. Again, the actual location of the early post office was moved with different postmasters. The site was not officially changed with the government until later.

Like many of the other post offices, the location of mail services at Phippsburg moved with the post masters.[190] At least one place that the Phippsburg residents could obtain their letters was at Sam Iacovetto's

The winter mail delivery sled to Pinnacle, 1927. *Herold family collection.*

General Store; Sam's son, Raymond, was postmaster. When the store closed, the post office was moved up the road about one hundred yards to its present location. Ray Iacovetto remained the postmaster for several more years.

The small rural post offices had the mail delivered by rural contractors. Sometimes, the mail for the Pinnacle Post Office was delivered from Yampa and at others it was delivered from Hayden.

CHURCHES

From the time that the first homesteaders settled in the Egeria Park area, there were church services of one kind or another. The first services were held in the homestead cabins. Sometimes a visiting preacher would pass through the valley; at other times a few families would get together and read the Bible. In a few years, many of the homesteaders started meeting in the building on First Street that is now the Masonic lodge.

In 1902, Jim Norvell challenged his congregation to raise enough money to build a church on Moffat Avenue. They did, and it was completed except for the bell tower by the end of the year. The first sermon in the new building was for the Christmas services. The bell tower was completed the following summer. This was a Congregational church; it is still in use as a church but is now a nondenominational church known as the Yampa Bible Church.

In the 1930s, the Nazarene congregation decided to build a church on Main Street. This log church was quite active for several years, but in the 1980s, the building was sold and is now used as a private residence. One story told about that church:

> *The bell was bought from the town of Yampa. It had been used as the town's fire bell. The town no longer needed that bell as they had started using a siren. The Nazarenes started ringing that bell every Sunday morning; once an hour before service began and again just as the service started. On Sunday mornings many people jumped out of bed in alarm as they still thought of that distinctive sound as a fire bell.*

The third church building in Yampa was the "Red Church." When the Southern Baptists built their church on Main Street, it was painted red. Even after the building was refinished in a different color, the people of Yampa

The Congregational church, pictured here in 1977, is now the Yampa Bible Church. *Herold family collection.*

The Church of the Nazarene, pictured here about 1985, is now a private residence. *Herold family collection.*

Southern Baptist Church is informally known as the "Red Church." *Herold family collection.*

YAMPA VALLEY'S LOST EGERIA PARK

still called it the Red Church. This was to differentiate it from the "White Church" on Moffat Avenue.

Other religious denominations met and still meet in various homes throughout the area.

OTHER ENTERPRISES

The stores and other business establishments have undergone many different changes from the time that the first settlers arrived until now.

The first known building in what is now the town of Yampa was the cabin that became known as the VanCamp Cabins. The first recorded owner was Joe Ward. Ward possibly utilized an abandoned trapper's cabin. One of the interesting things about this building is the "gun ports" left between the logs. Ira VanCamp bought the homestead rights from Ward and lived at that location for many years.

C.A. "Judge" Morning had this to say about the town in March 1904:

> *Yampa has four general stores, two groceries, two saloons, two hotels, two livery stables, two black smith shops, two meat markets, one drug store, two harness shops, two real estate firms, four insurance agencies, one fine church building, one brick yard, one restaurant and rooming house, one shingle and feed mill, two surveyors, one newspaper and job outfit, four notaries public, two banks, one doctor, one lawyer, one United States commissioner, and the best graded school in the county.* [191]

The first store to be established was the Hernage Store in 1886. When he first started selling supplies and groceries to those early settlers, Henry Hernage operated out of a small one-room cabin. He kept adding onto the size of his building until he had an imposing two-story structure that served several different purposes. Groceries and supplies were still sold. The Stockman's Bank was located in one portion of the building. The Masonic Lodge met upstairs in the large open room there. At different times, living quarters were also maintained upstairs.

Later, this building was sold to Lawrence E. Ochampaugh. He sold farm implements, machinery, parts and supplies, as well as general merchandise. The name Ochampaugh's was painted prominently on the building along with a large John Deere sign.

133

Sam Fix started the next general store; before 1889, Fix's opened on the west end of Moffat Avenue to compete with the Hernage Store. Fix carried all the general supplies needed by the early homesteaders. The goods were brought in from the railroad in Wolcott instead of the long haul from Denver; this cut down on both time and some of the cost of freight. At times, it was less expensive to haul bulky items directly from Denver.

Sam Fix soon sold his business to A.C. "Gus" Bower and A C.'s brother. At that time, the store changed its name to the Bower Brothers. Shortly after the sale, Agnes Amanda Fix married A.C. Bower in Salt Lake City, Utah. In 1914, the *Yampa Leader* reported "An Important Business Change" when A.C. Bower sold to Harry Kawin.[192] This building was known as the Yampa General Store during much of this time.

Kawin was the proprietor of the store for many years. By the 1940s, Joe and Mervin Montgomery owned the business; it has been owned by various members of the Montgomery family since that time. As of this writing, this establishment is the oldest continuously running general store in northwest Colorado.

From 1903 through 1910, Hernage, the Bell brothers, Buck and Son and Canant all owned or were concurrent partners in various stores. There were as many as six different grocery-type establishments open at the same time during those years. Some of them specialized in meat, some in groceries and some were general mercantiles.

The building, currently known as Crossan's M&A Market, was established by the Bell brothers and Canant in 1903. In 1906, the newspaper advertisements called it the Buck and Son General Merchandise Store, "Where you can get all Kinds of Fresh Meats, Fruits, Vegetables and the Best of Everything in groceries. We do all kinds of work in our Tin Shop. Make our Store your Home."[193] Buck and Moore became the owners in 1908. This building sold back to George Canant in 1909.

After the railroad arrived in 1908, the Bell brothers opened a second store in Oak Creek. Hernage moved to California, and his son retained the Moffat Avenue property. Canant kept the M & A Market building and also owned the Sanitary Market in Oak Creek. George Canant's daughter sold the store to Howard Allen and Joe Montgomery in 1935 when the name M&A Market was established. Joe Montgomery sold his share of the business in 1936. At that time, Bob Crossan joined Howard Allen in running the grocery store. These two fellows ran the store with the help of their wives, Lila and Florence, until Howard Allen decided to retire. George Crossan then joined his father, Bob, and the store remained in business until 1964.

The M & A Market, the second Bell brothers' store, can be seen on the left, circa 1940. *Courtesy of Yampa-Egeria Museum.*

Egeria Park had other stores, one in Toponas and three or four in Phippsburg. The Toponas store was a grocery store rather than a true general store. Jim Norvell opened it as a stage stop with rooms upstairs to serve as a hotel.[194] It never did carry a full line of dry goods or farm supplies. The first Toponas store was north of the railroad tracks on the original road. It wasn't until the 1940s that Jack Holden moved the store to its present location. At that time, the Toponas Post Office was inside the store and moved locations with the business.

In the early days of Phippsburg, there were several stores and pool halls in Phippsburg. When transportation to the nearby towns became easier, many of the small stores closed. The Iacovetto store remained in business. It carried not only supplies for the nearby homesteaders but also the basic needs for the railroad crews. It almost always carried a complete line of groceries and meats. The Sam Iacovetto family ran this establishment for many years.

The Charles P. Arnold family arrived in 1882. Charles started the first blacksmith shop in Egeria on the lot just south of the Sam Fix store.[195] The Arnolds lived in a house next to the shop.

There is some discrepancy over who was the first blacksmith in the area, as William Bird also claimed to be the first. It is likely they were both

Looking west on Moffat Avenue, the Arnold blacksmith shop is in the center, 1903. *Courtesy of Yampa-Egeria Museum, Fogg Collection.*

blacksmithing at the same time. With that many horses to be shod, wagon wheels that needed rims and plows to be sharpened and repaired, they were probably both busy.

Somewhere between 1900 and 1910, a fellow by the name French had a blacksmith shop, located on Moffat Avenue just east of the Van Camp buildings. It had a livery stable in the rear of the building. McClure bought this from French; at that time, French moved his operation to a building on the corner of Second Street and Main. Again, this had a blacksmith shop in front and a livery stable in the back. It later became Bob's Service Station. Owned by Bob Jones, it ran for nearly two decades. McClure ran the blacksmith business on Moffat Avenue until he built a house and shop on the corner of First Street and Clifton Avenue. Later, the shop on Clifton Avenue was owned by Wade Davis. In the early 1950s, Davis moved his business to a building on the south side of Moffat Avenue. During the 1950s, the high school used the McClure blacksmith building as a vocational shop.

The Yampa Creamery was established to make and sell butter and cheese. It was to be an outlet for surplus milk around early Yampa. In 1906, the *Yampa Leader* contained ads for the creamery. Jack Redmond stated that the beams under the floors of the building had a rather unusual construction

French's Blacksmith shop was on Moffat Avenue, photo about 1985. *Herold family collection.*

that was not the norm for the time.[196] But like many of the early enterprises in the valley, the creamery did not remain in business. By 1915, the building had become a residence.

The brick factory, built in 1908, was another early business. It was located about one and a half miles west of Yampa on what is now County Road 17. The owner erected his own private home with the bricks, but it was cheaper for most people to build their homes from logs or lumber. However, many of the chimneys around Egeria Park were constructed from those bricks. The brickmaker's house on Lincoln Street is the only known building made with local bricks that remains.

The Bank of Yampa was established in May 1903. The directors were Arnold Powell, F.A. Metcalf, Messre, Ashton, Fix, Van Dorn and Dart. That building, now the Yampa-Egeria Museum, was designed with a false front and a sloping shed roof. After the bank closed in the early 1930s, the Yampa Women's Club bought the building and converted it into a public library. The Town of Yampa acquired the building from the Ladies' Aid, and the library was moved next door. Both the exterior and the interior remain much as they were more than one hundred years ago. It is one of several structures in Yampa listed with Routt County as a historical building.

The Yampa Creamery was located on the corner of what is now County Road 17 and Roselawn Avenue, circa 1983. *Herold family collection.*

A house on Lincoln Avenue was made from local bricks, circa 1983. *Author's collection.*

The Bank of Yampa, pictured here in the 1950s, was built in 1903. It later housed a public library. *Courtesy of Yampa-Egeria Museum.*

The Stockman's Bank never had its own building in Yampa; it was on the ground floor of the Hernage building. This bank was an affiliate of the Stockman's Bank in Hayden.

The Antlers Hotel is at the south end of Main Street on Moffat Avenue. One of the more well-known buildings in Yampa, this was originally an impressive two-story hotel with a full upper balcony. When it was built in 1902, it was the largest hotel in Routt County. A paragraph in the *Yampa Leader* boasted:

> *Remember that the water used at the Antlers bath room is piped from a medicinal spring and has many health-giving properties. Mr. Colelesser has arranged this for hot or cold baths and has reduced the price to 35 cents for one bath or one dollar for a bath ticket which is good for four baths.* [197]

It is said that the Royal Hotel was inspired by Teddy Roosevelt Jr., who came into Egeria Park on a hunting trip in 1900 and wanted a hunting lodge in Yampa. He (or someone) apparently came up with the money, because T. P. and Lem Lindsey built the west wing in 1903. The rest of the building

The Stockman's Bank inside the Hernage Store, circa 1920. *Courtesy of Yampa-Egeria Museum, Fogg Collection.*

was finished a couple years after that and was connected by a large balcony overlooking Moffat Avenue. Lem and his wife, Minni, ran the hotel for many years. Roosevelt never came back to visit the Royal Hotel, but a variety of other historical figures did, including Zane Gray, Butch Cassidy and, of course, its resident ghost, Rufus. The building with all its visual impact burned down in 2015.

The Yampa Saloon, on the corner of Main Street and Moffat Avenue, was built about 1900. It remained a saloon until Prohibition. In the 1930s, Billy Macfarlane turned the building diagonally with Moffat Avenue and Main Street.[198] This was to serve as a gas station with two gas pumps erected in front for easy access. Since that time, the building has served as a post office, a hardware store, a laundromat and a beauty salon—thus, the evolution of a building from a saloon to a salon.

Another prominent building on Moffat Avenue during the 1940s was the M&M Garage. Billy Macfarlane and Elmer Margerum had a garage and sold gasoline at the pumps in front. This building had many different additions

The Antlers Hotel. *Pictured here are, from left to right (top):* Myrtie Bird Trantham, Levi Trantham, Minnie Lindsey, Addie Hunter and unidentified; *(bottom)* Ida Bird, Annie Butteric, Harry Butteric, Annie Hopper *(in the window)*, Alice Bird, Leash Cottening, Lem Lindsey, Auntie Lindsey, J.P. Lindsey, Emma Bryand, Maud Trantham, Dan Trantham, Gus Bowers and Etta Phillips. *Herold family collection.*

The Royal Hotel was the backdrop for the Fourth of July broom polo game, 2010. *Author's collection.*

Left: The Yampa Leader Building on Main Street when Eugene Godfrey was editor, circa 1920. *Courtesy of Yampa-Egeria Museum, Fogg Collection.*

Below: The Masonic Hall on First Street, 2006. *Author's collection.*

after it was first built in the early 1900s. Each addition had progressively lower ceilings as the roof sloped toward the south.

The *Yampa Leader* newspaper was first distributed on May 30, 1903; V.S. Wilson was editor. By 1914, Eugene Godfrey was the editor. The news and events of the Egeria Park were reported in its pages and read by most of the residents. It was published from at least two different buildings in Yampa: a small building in the one hundred block on Main Street and in a corner of the building known as the Royal Hotel. The *Yampa Leader* remained a weekly newspaper for many years. In its final years, it was published (still by Eugene Godfrey) in Oak Creek along with the *Oak Creek Times*.

The Ladies Aid Hall started its life on Moffat Avenue in 1902. Isaac Bijou obtained a grocery license from the clerk at Hahn's Peak for the building he had recently put up. This building also had several owners during the next few years. It saw service as a grocery store, a restaurant and a saloon. It was then moved from Moffat Avenue to its present location on First Street. The Woodsmen of the World then refitted the building for use as a lodge. After that, it saw use as a movie theater and dance hall. In 1925, the Yampa Ladies Aid incorporated so it could legally own property and buy the building.

The Masonic Hall located on First Street looks almost exactly as it did when it was erected. It was built about 1891. In its early days, it too saw many different uses. It served as a church, a community hall and for a time became an opera house. The bottom floor served as a public room for the school; it wasn't until after the new two-story brick school was built that the programs were held in the school.[199] Before that, there was not enough room in any of the classrooms to hold everyone for the Christmas pageants or end-of-school programs. For a number of years after the Masonic Lodge obtained the building, the lower floor was still used for public events, such as dances or movies. It is still owned and used as a Masonic Lodge.

Some early dates of interest to the history of the Egeria Park area and to Yampa include:

1883   The first post office is established in Egeria Park.
1886   The Town of Egeria changes its name to Yampa.
1886   The first school is established in Egeria Park.
1886   The first store (the Hernage Store) opens across Moffat Avenue from VanCamp's.
1886   The first county road is built along the valley.
1891   The Woodsmen of the World lodge is established in Yampa.

1902   The Congregational church is built.
1903   The *Yampa Leader* newspaper is started on May 30.
1906   Yampa is incorporated as a town on April 17.
1906   The Colorado Telephone company is franchised.
1908   The tracks for the Moffat Railroad reach Yampa.
1909   The Town of Yampa acquires the Yampa Cemetery site.
1910   The Yampa water system with the wooden water mains is installed.

Many of the businesses in Egeria Park have come and gone. Some of the buildings have survived the wearing of time to give us a glimpse into a former era. You might want to take a slow walk through Egeria Park, look at the buildings and listen for the ghosts of the past to tell their stories.

NOTES

Chapter 1

1. Gray, *Recollections*.
2. Hometown Locater, http://colorado.hometownlocator.com.
3. "Egeria," Stargate Wiki, http://www.stargate-sg1-solutions.com/wiki/Egeria.
4. Gray, *Recollections*.
5. Leslie, *Anthracite, Barbee and Tosh*, 46.
6. Moore, interview, June 10, 1999.
7. Bancroft, *Colorful Colorado*.
8. Chapman, *Story of Colorado*.
9. Smith, *With Fur Traders*.
10. Flora, "Journey of the Peoria Party."
11. "First Tourist Visited in Steamboat 95 Years Ago," *Steamboat Pilot*, July 9, 1934.
12. Favour, *Old Bill Williams*.
13. *Daily Ohio State Journal*, June 20, 1854.
14. Roberts, *Amazing Adventures*.
15. "First Settlers Here Always a Mystery," *Steamboat Pilot*, July 27, 1934, 2.
16. Pritchett, *Maggie by My Side*.
17. Metcalf and Downey, *Colorado*, 135.
18. Hafen and Hafen, *Colorado Story*, 257–61.
19. Chapman, *Story of Colorado*, 81–86.
20. FitzPatrick, *Red Twilight*.
21. Metcalf and Downey, *Colorado*, 133.
22. Ibid., 125.
23. Whipple, letter to the editor, September 14, 1941.
24. "Scraps of History–Tales of the Old West," *Steamboat Pilot*, December 23, 1937.

25. Gray, *Recollections*.
26. Moore, "Some Things I Have Been Told." These and other unpublished manuscripts are in the author's collection.
27. Neiman, "Crossans."
28. Moore, "Some Things I Have Been Told."

Chapter 2

29. Gray, *Recollections*.
30. Whipple, letter.
31. "Routt-Moffat Pioneer Picnic," *Steamboat Pilot*, July 7, 1933.
32. Ibid.
33. Gray, *Recollections*.
34. Ibid.
35. Ibid.
36. Moore, "Some Things I Have Been Told."
37. Wilson, *Mother Remembers*.
38. Ibid.
39. Gray, *Recollections*.

Chapter 3

40. Pritchett, *Maggie by My Side*.
41. Wilson, *Mother Remembers*, 12–13.
42. Gray, *Recollections*.
43. Moore, "More Memories and Thoughts."
44. *Yampa Leader*, January 6, 1905, 4.
45 "A.C. Bower Purchases Automobile," *Yampa Leader*, May 23, 1913, 1.
46. Wilson, *Mother Remembers*.
47. Moore, "Some Things I Have Been Told."
48. "Stage Drivers Met Difficulties in Concord Coach Days," *Steamboat Pilot*, July 27, 1934, 4.
49. Ibid.
50. Morning, "Yampa on the Bear."
51. Nay, *There Was Always a Sam*.
52. "Moffat Rails Reach Town," *Yampa Leader*, August 1, 1908, 1.
53. "First Train to Yampa on Monday," *Yampa Leader*, September 12, 1908.
54. "First Passenger Train," *Yampa Leader*, September 19, 1908, 1.
55. *Historical Guide to Routt County*.
56. Hamidy, "Letter to Mrs. Lenore Holthouse."
57. Hamidy, "Personal Note."

58. Shockley, "Shorty Hamidy."
59. Herold, interview with the author.
60. Moore, "Few More Thoughts."

Chapter 4

61. Moore, interview, June 9, 1999.
62. Moore, "Few More Thoughts."
63. Ibid.
64. *Yampa Leader*, October 7, 1905.
65. Moore, "Some Things I Have Been Told."
66. Moore, interview, July 2004.
67. Moore, interview, August 1993.
68. Moore, interview, August 2004.
69. Moore, interview, February 18, 2006.
70. Moore, interview, 1993.
71. Moore, interview, May 27, 2000.
72. *Yampa Leader*, September 2, 1905, 4.
73. Ibid.
74. *Yampa Leader*, September 9, 1905, 4.
75. "The Northwestern Colorado," supplement to the *Steamboat Pilot* by the Federated Commercial Clubs of Northwestern Colorado, June 18, 1924. Promotional/informational supplement of the *Steamboat Pilot*. A copy can be found at the Museum of Northwest Colorado in Craig, CO.
76. "Splendid Prospects for Good Head Lettuce Crop in the Yampa Valley," *Steamboat Pilot*, June 16, 1922.
77. Moore, "Few Comical Incidents from My Memory."
78. Moore, interview, August 2005.
79. Moore, "Some Answers."
80. "Ice House for Yampa Lettuce Packing," *Yampa Leader*, June 13, 1924.
81. "Espy Ice Sheds," An Inventory of Historical Sites. According to Katy Adams at the Tread of Pioneers, the research for this was probably done in the 1980s; the manuscript has been taken apart and put into separate categories at the Tread of the Pioneers Museum in Steamboat.
82. Redmond, "Yampa's Lettuce."
83. Moore, interview, September 9, 2004.
84. Moore, interview, August 2005; Moore, "Few Comical Incidents."
85. Yurich, interview, August 2005.
86. Mohr, "Autobiography." The Yampa-Egeria Museum has a copy.
87. McCoy, "Margaret Rossi."
88. Moore, interview, August 18, 2005.

89. Moore, "Few Comical Incidents."

90. Wellenkotter, "Lettuce Shipping Operations."

91. "Colorado's Spinach King," *Rocky Mountain Empire*, August 11, 1946, 2.

92. *Yampa Leader*, July 1, 1905, 1.

93. *Yampa Leader*, October 7, 1905, 4.

94. Ibid.

95. Moore, interview, June 19, 2004.

96. Ibid.

97. Pidcock, interview, June 2000.

98. Ibid.

99. Moore, interview, August 18, 2005.

100. Mohr, "Autobiography."

101. Cole, journal.

102. Moore, "Some Things I Have Been Told."

103. Crossan, "Pioneer of South Routt County Colorado."

Chapter 5

104. "Birth of a Town—Yampa Turns 85," *Steamboat Pilot*, May 9, 1991, section D.

105. Mauch, *Yampa Bible Church*.

106. *Yampa Leader*, August 16, 1905, 4.

107. Moore, "Greenridge Tales."

108. Viele, "Early Logging Camps and Sawmills on the Hunt Creek Drainage." The Tracks and Trails Museum in Oak Creek has a copy.

109. Ibid.

110. Ibid.

111. Moore, "Some Answers."

112. Moore, interview, September 4, 1999.

113. Moore, "Few More Thoughts."

114. Moore, "Some Answers."

115. Ibid.

116. Moore, "Still More Memories of Days Gone By."

117. Moore, "Some Answers."

118. Moore, interview, July 17, 2005.

119. Moore, interview, May 6, 2006.

120. Moore, interview, April 8, 2008.

121. Moore, interview, July 5, 2004.

122. Moore, interview, June 24, 2005.

123. Moore, interview, June 22, 2003.

124. Moore, interview, June 24, 2005.

125. Ibid.

126. Moore, "Greenridge Tales."
127. Ibid.
128. Whaley, interview.
129. Moore, interview, August 25, 2005.
130. Mohr, "Autobiography."
131. Moore, interview, June 25, 2003.
132. Moore, interview, July 2004.
133. Maijala, "Maijala Family of Yampa."
134. Maijala, "Micket Remembers."
135. Moore, interview, July 2004.
136. Ray, "Sawmills in Toponas."
137. Ibid.
138. Ibid.
139. Ibid.
140. Ibid.
141. Ibid.
142. Curtis, oral communication.
143. Ray, "Sawmills in Toponas."

Chapter 6

144. Pritchett, *Crawford Pioneer Tales*, 15.
145. Whipple, letter.
146. "Vast Cattle Herds Grazed in County," *Steamboat Pilot*, July 1959, 6B.
147. Crossan, "Pioneer of South Routt County Colorado."
148. "Yampa Is One Town," *Steamboat Pilot*, July 30, 1964, 4B.
149. Long, oral communication, April 2005.
150. Moore, "Few More Thoughts."
151. Wilson, *Mother Remembers*.
152. Moore, "Some Things I Have Been Told."
153. Carpenter, *Confessions of a Maverick*.
154. *History of Routt National Forest*, 47.
155. Athearn, *Isolated Empire*, 78.
156. "Riding the Range," *Steamboat Pilot*, November 1, 1979.
157. Moore, interview, June 23, 2003.
158. Moore, "More Thoughts from Years Gone By."
159. Moore, interview, July 4, 2005.
160. Moore, "More Memories and Thoughts."
161. Moore, "More Thoughts from Years Gone By."
162. Ibid.

Chapter 7

163. "Story of Routt County's Early Schools," *Steamboat Pilot*, July 30, 1959, 8B.

164. "Egeria Items," *Yampa Leader*, July 8, 1905, 4.

165. Leslie, *Routt County Rural Schools*.

166. Wilson, *Mother Remembers*, 52.

167. Rockhill, "My Life Story," 6.

168. Leslie, *Routt County Rural Schools*.

169. Moore, interview, January 2006.

170. Leslie, *Routt County Rural Schools*.

171. Redmond, interview.

172. "Yampa, South Routt Community," *Steamboat Pilot*, April 15, 1976, 2-A.

173. *Oak Creek Times*, May 10, 1911.

174. Moore, "Some Things I Have Been Told."

175. Moore, interview, June 1999.

176. Ibid.

177. Moore, interview, June 18, 2003.

178. Moore, interview, July 2004.

179. "Scraps of History," *Steamboat Pilot*, December 23, 1937.

180. Moore, "Some Things I Have Been Told."

181. "Birth of a Town," *Steamboat Pilot*, May 9, 1991, section D-1.

182. Wilson, *Mother Remembers*, 52.

183. Leslie, *Anthracite, Barbee, and Tosh*.

184. Wilson, *Mother Remembers*, 52.

185. Leslie, *Anthracite, Barbee, and Tosh*.

186. *Yampa Leader*, November 28, 1903, 4.

187. Ibid.

188. Ibid.

189. *Yampa Leader*, July 4, 1908. p. 8.

190. Leslie, *Anthracite, Barbee, and Tosh*.

191. Morning, "Yampa on the Bear."

192. "Important Business Change for Yampa," *Yampa Leader*, March 13, 1914. p. 1.

193. Advertisement, *Yampa Leader*, 1906.

194. Leslie, *Anthracite, Barbee, and Tosh*.

195. "Birth of a Town."

196. Redmond, interview.

197. *Yampa Leader*, September 9, 1905.

198. Moore, interview, June 18, 2003.

199. Moore, interview, July 2004.

BIBLIOGRAPHY

Athearn, Frederic. J. *An Isolated Empire: History of Northwest Colorado*. Denver, CO: Bureau of Land Management, 1976.

Bancroft, Caroline. *Colorful Colorado*. Denver, CO: Sage Books, 1959.

Carpenter, Farrington R. *Confessions of a Maverick*. Denver: State Historical Society of Colorado, 1984.

Chapman, Arthur. *The Story of Colorado*. New York: Rand McNally, 1925.

Cole, Ruth. Journal, unpub. 1948–1953. Yampa-Egeria Museum.

Colorado: A History of the Centennial State. Boulder: Colorado University Press, 1982.

Crossan, George Charles. "Pioneer of South Routt County Colorado—George Cooke Crossan." Unpublished manuscript, 2000.

Curtis, Ron. Oral communication with the author, February 2019.

Daily Ohio State Journal. June 20, 1854.

Favour, Alpheus H. *Old Bill Williams—Mountain Man*. Norman: University of Oklahoma Press, 1936.

FitzPatrick, Val. *Red Twilight, The Last Free Days of the Ute Indians*. Moab, UT: Yellow Cat Publishing, 1999.

Flora, Stephanie. "Journey of the Peoria Party." Oregon Pioneers, oregonpioneers.com/peoria.htm.

Gray, David S. *Recollections of an Egeria Park Pioneer*. Steamboat Springs, CO: Steamboat Pilot, 1941.

Hafen, LeRoy, and Ann Hafen. *Colorado Story*. Denver, CO: Old West Publishing, 1954.

Hamidy, Tirzah Sheppard. "Letter to Mrs. Lenore Holthouse" *Oak Creek Memories* 3 (1997).

———. "Personal Note." *Oak Creek Memories* (1982).

Herold, Carl W., Sr. Interview with the author, October 1963.

Historical Guide to Routt County. Steamboat Springs, CO: Tread of the Pioneers Museum, 1979.

History of Routt National Forest, 1905–1972. N.p., 1973. https://lccn.loc.gov/74600848.

Leslie, Jan. *Anthracite, Barbee and Tosh: History of Routt County and Its Post Offices, 1875–1971.* Hayden, CO: Walnut St. Press, 2005.

———. *Routt County Rural Schools—Windows to Yesterday.* Steamboat Springs, CO: Legacy Books and Resources, 1998.

Long, Linda. Oral communication with the author, April 2005.

Maijala, Mickey. "Micket Remembers." Interview by Virginia Rossi, CNCC History and Legends, Fall 2005.

Maijala, Shellen. "The Maijala Family of Yampa." *South Routt Memories* 4 (2002).

Mauch, Elizabeth A., ed. *Yampa Bible Church, 100 Years of Memories, 1902–2002.* N.p.: Yampa Bible Church, 2002.

McCoy, Mark. "Margaret Rossi." *Three-Wire Winter* (Winter 1982).

Metcalf, Fay D., and Matthew T. Downey. *Colorado.* Boulder. CO: Pruett Publishing, 1986.

Mohr, Fred. "Autobiography." Undated. Yampa-Egeria Museum.

Moore, Francis. "A Few Comical Incidents from My Memory." 2001.

———. "A Few More Thoughts of Days Gone By." 2002.

———. "Greenridge Tales." September 1999.

———. Interviews by author, 1999–2008.

———. "More Memories and Thoughts." May 2002.

———. "More Thoughts from Years Gone By." June 2002.

———. "Some Answers." May 2002.

———. "Some Things I Have Been Told," 2002.

———. "Still More Memories of Days Gone By." June 2002.

Morning, C.A. "Yampa on the Bear." *Steamboat Pilot,* March 2, 1904.

Nay, Samuel, Jr. *There Was Always a Sam.* Garden Grove, CA: Keepsake Publishing, 2004.

Neiman, Ruby. "The Crossans." Unpub. manuscript. Undated.

Pidcock, Evelyn. Interview by author, June 2000.

Pritchett, Lulita Crawford. *Crawford Pioneer Tales.* Steamboat Springs, CO: Tread of the Pioneers Museum, 2005.

———. *Maggie by My Side.* Hot Sulphur Springs, CO: Grand County Historical Association, 1983.

Ray, Janet. "Sawmills in Toponas and Near Vicinity." Manuscript for CNCC History and Legends, Fall 2005.

Redmond, Jack. Interview with the author, December 2011.

Redmond, Wanda. "Yampa's Lettuce." Presentation at Brown Bag Lunch, Tread of Pioneers Museum, 2007.

Roberts, Jack. *The Amazing Adventures of Lord Gore, a True Saga from the Old West.* Silverton, CO: Sundance Books, 1977.

Rockhill, Clayton. "My Life Story." Unpublished manuscript, 1991.

Rocky Mountain Empire. "Colorado's Spinach King." August 11, 1946.

Shockley, Kellie. "Shorty Hamidy, Don't Let Him Quit that Store, It's Part of His Life." *Three Wire Winter* (Spring 1981).

Smith, Willard E. *With Fur Traders in Colorado, 1839–1840*. Franklin, TN: Territorial Press, 1888.

Steamboat Pilot. "Birth of a Town—Yampa Turns 85." May 9, 1991.

———. "First Settlers Here Always a Mystery." July 27, 1934.

———. "First Tourist Visited in Steamboat 95 Years Ago." July 9, 1934.

———. "Riding the Range with a Routt Pioneer." November 1, 1979.

———. "Routt-Moffat Pioneer Picnic." July 7, 1933.

———. "Scraps of History—Tales of the Old West." December 23, 1937.

———. "Splendid Prospects for Good Head Lettuce Crop in the Yampa Valley— Colorado Head Lettuce Is the Best in the World." June 16, 1922.

———. "Stage Drivers Met Difficulties in Concord Coach Days." July 27, 1934.

———. "Story of Routt County's Early Schools Is Story of Emma Peck." July 30, 1959.

———. "Vast Cattle Herds Grazed in County." July 9, 1959.

———. "Yampa Is One Town that Grew Up Naturally." July 30, 1964.

———. "Yampa, South Routt Community One Hundred Years Young." April 15, 1976.

Viele, Floyd "Dutch." "Early Logging Camps and Sawmills on the Hunt Creek Drainage," Interview by Virginia Rossi, CNCC History and Legends, Fall 2005.

Wellenkotter, Jack. "Lettuce Shipping Operations in Full Swing at C.E. Crowner & Sons Plant." *Steamboat Pilot*, August 30, 1951.

Whaley, Blaine Dale. Interview by Carol Villa. CNCC History and Legends, Spring 2005.

Whipple, Don Wilmer (Billy). Letter to the editor. *Steamboat Pilot*, September 14, 1941.

Wilson (King), May. *Mother Remembers*. Steamboat Springs, CO: Steamboat Pilot, 1973.

Yampa Leader. "A.C. Bower Purchases Automobile." May 23, 1913.

———. "Egeria Items." July 8, 1905.

———. "First Passenger Train." September 19, 1908.

———. "First Train to Yampa on Monday." September 12, 1908.

———. "Ice House for Yampa Lettuce Packing." June 13, 1924.

———. "Important Business Change for Yampa." March 13, 1914.

———. "Moffat Rails Reach Town." August 1, 1908.

Yurich, Mike. Interview with the author, August 2005.

INDEX

ABOUT THE AUTHOR

Rita Herold is a descendant of early settlers and pioneers of Routt County. She and her family live on and operate a fifth-generation centennial ranch near Yampa, Colorado. As she grew up listening to the stories of the area told by her father, grandfathers and great-uncles, her passion for history developed at an early age.

Rita graduated from Utah State University with a bachelor's degree in education. She taught grades kindergarten through twelfth and worked as an adjunct history teacher for both Colorado Northwestern Community College and Colorado Mountain College. Rita has given numerous talks and lectures for the Tread of Pioneers Museum, Tracks and Trails Museum and the Yampa–Egeria Museum. She has developed history tours of southern Routt County and history curriculums for students.

With community in mind, Rita has served as a longtime 4-H leader and Routt County Fair volunteer. She has been a board member and volunteer in the Cattle Women's Association, Routt County Preservation Board and the Yampa–Egeria Historical Society.

Rita enjoys writing, art, photography, traveling and her family. She is currently working on her second book.

www.ingramcontent.com/pod-product-compliance
Lightning Source LLC
Chambersburg PA
CBHW040135270326
41927CB00019B/3395